WILL
POWER

**sound
wisdom.**
Because Your Success Matters

WILL POWER

UNLOCKING THE HIDDEN FORCE THAT DRIVES SUCCESS

WILLIAM WALKER ATKINSON

"An act of will is what makes people change themselves for the better."

—EARL NIGHTINGALE

First published in 1922 by William Walker Atkinson.

Reprint edition by Sound Wisdom, 2025

Cover design and interior page design, copyright 2019. All rights reserved.

ISBN 13 TP: 978-1-64095-589-9

ISBN 13 eBook: 978-1-64095-590-5

1 2 3 4 5 6 7 8 / 29 28 27 26 25

CONTENTS

CHAPTER 1

WILLPOWER

Of all the varied manifestations of power proceeding from that Power which the best human thought perceives to be the source and origin of all the power in the universe, that manifestation we know as willpower seems to be the most fundamental, the most elemental, the most universal. It is seen by philosophers to constitute the very kernel or heart of all phases and forms of personal power. Many, indeed, have held that in willpower abides the ultimate principle of the universe—and that all forms of power, force, and energy must be thought of in terms of willpower.

Whatever may be the ultimate facts of the universe, there can be no dispute concerning the dominating position occupied by willpower in the life and being of the individual person. When you undertake the task of self-analysis, you will find your will at the very center of your being—so close to the "I AM I," or ego, that it is most difficult to disentangle it from your real self.

Your sensations, your passions, your emotions, your tastes, and your talents are found to be under the control of your trained will. You may set them aside from yourself and analyze them, correct them, improve them; but the will lies closer to yourself—you cannot set it apart from yourself as you can the other mental states. It is neither sensation nor emotion—though it may dominate both. It is always subjective and active, abiding and operating from the very citadel of your being.

Emotion and thought may lie deep in your being—but will lies still deeper. Emotion and thought are objective to the will, and may be influenced and directed by it. You are conscious of your sensations and of your emotions as merely incidental to your existence. But you are directly conscious of your will, just as you are conscious of your self-existence. You can modify your other mental states, but you cannot modify your will in the same way; the will is your sole instrument of modification and it cannot be turned back on itself. The office of the will is that of action, and in its activities it directs and orders, commands, and regulates the other mental states. In fact, the will acts chiefly through and by means of its control and direction of your other mental states.

Willpower may be developed and trained, of course—otherwise this book would have no purpose. But it is not to be developed and trained as are the other mental states or powers—for these are modified by the action of the will upon them. Unlike theirs, the will's development consists rather of the unfolding into fuller expression of a fundamental power that already exists—the transformation of latent and static will into active and dynamic will. This form of "development" is defined as "the act of freeing from that which envelopes." Its training, likewise, is different. Instead of its being trained by a higher mental faculty or power, the will itself proceeds to improve, deepen, widen, and strengthen the channels through which its currents flow. We, therefore, employ the term *the development and training of the will* only in this sense.

Will culture really is the process of providing the will with the appropriate mental instruments for its fuller expression and manifestation, and of encouraging it to employ them. The will always is there, abiding in full power. It is your part to supply it with the proper incentives to action and to furnish it with the channels of habit and use through which it may flow freely. Strange to say, you must employ the powers of will itself in order to provide these requisites for its own fuller expression. At the last, the will itself must "will" to provide itself with the instruments of willing. The will must will to will—and to will into being the instruments of its future willing. But the will is always content to do these things when properly aroused.

I need not labor to convince you that it is desirable for you to possess developed and trained willpower. You know from your own experience and observation that to have "a strong will" is to be a strong individual—one who is regarded with respect. You know also that to have a "weak will" is to be a weak individual—one to be pitied, if not scorned. You may, however, have fallen into the error of supposing that the possessors of the "strong will" are individuals especially favored and blessed by nature, or by the powers above nature. You may be among those who regard strength of will as akin to height, complexion, or similar personal characteristics that have been bestowed upon certain individuals without any effort on their part, and to which no other individuals may hope to attain if they have not been born with them.

If you have fallen into this error, now is the time for you to rid yourself of it. Thoughtful psychologists take an entirely different view of the case. While recognizing the fact that to some individuals the manifestation of willpower is easier at the beginning—that it "comes more natural" to some than to others, those who have made a careful study of this subject know that it is equally true that each and every individual has a bountiful supply of latent willpower which they may develop and train to a marvelous degree if they will employ the proper scientific methods. In fact, experience has proved that many of the individuals who have acquired a high degree of willpower are able to manifest it more consistently and more habitually than many of those who were "born to it" but who have not learned how to apply it effectively.

It is true that in order to develop and train your willpower, you will need to arouse and apply a certain degree of will itself—you will also find that your willpower, once set into operation in this direction, will rise to the occasion, and that your supply of such power will prove to be equal to your demands upon it. One may start with even a far less degree of willpower than that possessed by the average person, and then proceed step by step in attainment and development until the heights are reached. Accompanying the very application of willpower to the task of developing itself by special training, there is a correlated arousing of its latent energies; the employment of willpower in this effort tends to strengthen and energize its power of manifestation in other directions.

I ask you to take careful notice of this peculiar situation. Willpower may be developed and trained only by willpower. Willpower is required to develop and to train willpower. Willpower is self-developed and self-trained. Willpower applies its energies to itself, and by means of this it tends to perfect and improve itself. The other mental faculties and powers find it necessary to call on willpower to perfect them; but willpower requires no outside aid and can obtain none—it must ever fall back upon its own inherent powers when it wishes to develop or improve itself. If you had no willpower, you would never be able to develop any—since you would have nothing else with which to develop it. But fortunately, you have will to start with, though it may exist merely in a latent or dormant state. Willpower is your heritage, and it will be at your service if you demand it.

When you employ willpower to develop willpower, you not only build a mental path for the will to travel, but you also actually strengthen and develop the will itself by the very task of building such paths or roads. In creating the tools for the use of the will, you also render the will itself stronger, better, and more efficient. Here we have a striking illustration of the old biblical statement: "Whoever has will be given more, and they will have an abundance." The more persistent and the longer continued the efforts of your will to develop and train your willpower, the stronger your will becomes by reason of the energies expended in the effort.

By employing willpower in the task, you will actually gain willpower as the result. This is a very significant fact, and one which you should always bear in mind. The more of will you give, the more of will you have—this is the way of the will!

Here at the very beginning, you should realize that there is no royal road to the development and training of willpower. There is no magic charm that will transform the weak-willed individual into the strong-willed one. There is no miraculous drug, concealed in an attractive capsule, which needs but to be swallowed in order to render you a veritable Sampson or Napoleon of willpower. There is no magician's wand which may transform you in the twinkling of an eye into a person with the will of a Titan. Those who have dreamed of such a miraculous and magic processes of transformation may as well realize these facts right here at the beginning.

But equally true is it that the wonderful results that many have dreamed of securing are attainable, provided that you will apply yourself to the task in the right spirit and with a firm determination to succeed. You may obtain the highest success in this direction, but you must work for it just as you must work for anything else worthwhile in life. Just as you may develop yourself physically by exercise, so you may develop your willpower by scientific methods and exercises. This, indeed, is the only way. Willpower may be obtained in no other way. But, on the other hand, the reward will far more than repay you for your efforts; moreover, once you have taken the first few steps, you will find that your interest will increase, and you will be encouraged by the many little indications of the actual development of willpower that will make themselves manifest even from the start.

I would here call your attention to another important and interesting fact concerning the task of the development and training of willpower. While the discipline and exercise of the task entails some degree of self-sacrifice as you set aside certain minor habits, you will find yourself more than compensated for the loss by the pleasure which comes from the unfolding of new powers within yourself. The new interests will soon supplant the old ones, and the joy of possession will overbalance the price of denial.

In this connection, I would impress upon you the fact that no intelligent application of willpower is a loss—such is always a gain. In every intelligent exercise or application of the will you are making an investment in willpower—you are making a deposit in the bank of will, and this bank pays at an attractive rate of interest. I know of no better investment for you. Your expenditures are transformed into savings stored up as a reserve fund drawing good interest. This surely should prove an attractive proposition for you.

I take it that you have already developed at least the average degree of willpower. The fact that you have undertaken the study of this book is evidence that you have developed at least some degree of "the will to will"—that you know what a valuable thing willpower is, and that you desire to possess and manifest still more of it. I am proceeding upon such an assumption, even when I may seem to be giving instruction designed for those of a lesser degree of attainment. Do not make the mistake of passing over any of the simple and elementary phases of this instruction merely because you may think that you have passed beyond that stage and outgrown the need for such instruction. The rule is this: That which will make a weak will strong will make a strong will stronger. Even the most elementary method or exercise may be employed profitably by those of giant willpower, particularly where the strength has not been effectively trained or efficiently directed.

If you are seeking, by the methods of this book, to direct the efforts of some weaker-willed friend or relation, I would say that you are on the right road. There are no exceptions to the rule that willpower can be developed and trained in any individual. While there is will, there is hope. There is latent will in everyone—even in the weakest-willed person. Moreover, those who are suffering from a diseased will, or from a discouraged will, may feel certain that the right effort will raise them from their unfortunate condition. There lives no person to whom the benefit of will culture is denied. There is no person so weak, so old, so burdened with a long series of will-failures to whom it cannot be said truthfully, "The gate of hope is still open to you; enter into your own kingdom of awakened will!"

Now, right here at the beginning of our instruction, I shall ask you to recall an experience of your youth—if you have ever lived in the country, you will understand the principle involved. I allude to the process whereby the good old pump on the farm was "set a-going" by means of the process of "priming" it—pouring into the pump a pailful of water in order to set into operation the internal mechanism whereby the working of the pump-handle brought up to the spout a free and full supply of water. Now, then, here at this point we are going to ask you to "prime" your good pump of willpower in order to "set it a-going." Later, you will find some good suggestions concerning that which you should pour into the pump of willpower in the process of "priming" it. Pour these in, and before long you will feel the thrill of the mounting willpower—the will to will.

PRIMING THE PUMP OF WILLPOWER

Ponder

Begin by realizing just how much you really want to attain strong and effective willpower. Let the feelings of your subconscious mentality rise to the surface of your consciousness. You will discover that you have some very strong feelings on the subject—give to these feelings the full possession of your mind. Let the desire for willpower permeate your whole being. Do not rest satisfied until you want willpower as the drowning person wants air, as the starving person wants food, as the thirsting person wants water, as the wild creature wants its mate, as the mother creature wants its young. Before you can get anything, you must "want it hard enough."

Picture

Picture yourself in imagination as already possessed of strong willpower. See yourself, in mental pictures, as manifesting the actions of the person of giant will. See yourself as the person of invincible determination— of the purpose once fixed, and then victory or death. See yourself as the person possessed of that strong and indefatigable will which treads down difficulties and dangers as the boy treads down the frozen snow in winter. See yourself as possessed of that settled purpose which demands fulfillment and will not be denied. See yourself as possessed of that passionate and unwearied will which performs that which seems impossible to the eyes of the cold and feeble. See yourself as the person who will not yield to the casualties of life, but who forces them to yield to you; who compels circumstances to serve your purposes and designs, though they had at first seemed determined to frustrate you. See yourself as possessed of that spirit of will, that firm, decisive spirit, which clears a space around you and leaves you room and freedom for action. Memorize and ponder over the following lines from Ella Wheeler Wilcox:

"*There is no chance, no destiny, no fate,*

Can circumvent, or hinder, or control

The firm resolve of a determined soul.

Gifts count for nothing, will alone is great;

All things give way before it soon or late.

What obstacles can stay the mighty force

Of the sea-seeking river in its courseOr cause
    the ascending orb of day to wait?

Each well-born soul must win what it deserves.

Let the fools prate of luck. The fortunate

Is he whose earnest purpose never swerves,

Whose slightest action or inactionServes
    the one great aim.

Why, even Death itself

Stands still and waits an hour sometimes

For such a will."

Pay the Price

Next, carefully consider the question of whether or not you are ready and willing to pay the price of effort, exercise, and training necessary for the attainment of strong willpower. Proceed honestly in this matter; do not try to deceive yourself. Weigh carefully the advantages that will accrue to you as the result of your attainment of the qualities and powers seen in the mental picture you have just considered. Against these, balance the degree of work, time, attention, and the general mental discipline you must perform as the price of your attainment. Balance the "goods" against the "price," and decide whether or not you will get full value for your money.

You must settle this question once and for all, right here at the beginning—you must not carry it over into the later stages of this instruction, there to plague and torment you. If you find that you are not willing to pay the price, all well and good—in such case close this book and dismiss the subject from your mind. Leave it for some more courageous and determined soul. But if, as we anticipate, you decide that "the game is worth the candle" and "the goods are cheap at the price," then close the contract with yourself and proceed as follows. Having fully "made up your mind," you should proceed to enter into the task of will development with *full determination and resolute purpose.* You must manifest not a mere passive or lukewarm resolve, but a real, red-blooded, virile resolution, which you are compelled to fulfill. You must will to will in this matter. You must throw the whole force of your being into the task of this *purposeful determination.* You must be prepared to act now in the manner in which you pictured yourself acting a few moments ago. You must burn your bridges behind you and enter upon the road from which there is no retreat.

Take as your battle cry, "I can, I will! I dare, I do!" Carry its inspiration with you. In your hours of struggle, effort, and battle against the forces of lethargy, apathy, inertia, and the tendency to "sidetrack" the decision, sound this note insistently and persistently. In your hours of discouragement, in which the tempter whispers in your ear, "What's the use?" set the vibrations of the battle cry into motion. Finally, in your hours of triumph, in which you enjoy your achievement with that keen pleasure that comes only to the one who has overcome obstacles by sheer persistence, determination, and will, let this be your vibrant note of victory!

Sound this note over and over again, until its vibrations energize every atom and cell of your being. Let its rhythm awaken the thrill of willpower within you—until the "I can, I will! I dare, I do!" sounds from the very center of your being. Sound it over and over again, until you are fully conscious that its vibrations have begun and the whole mighty structure of your being is quivering and thrilling, throbbing and beating with the rhythmic vibration of the energy of your *persistent determination*—the spirit of your awakened will to will.

This, then, is the water of suggestive idea and mental imagery, of definite course and determined purpose, which you are pouring into your pump of will so as to "'prime" it and to "set it a-going"—and "set it a-going" it surely will!

CHAPTER 2

THE NATURE
OF WILL

Psychology finds itself confronted by a paradox when it undertakes the consideration of the will. While it is able to indicate clearly the several stages of the activity of will and also to point out positively the methods whereby the will may be developed and trained, yet when it seeks to indicate the essential nature of will it finds itself baffled at every turn and, in the end, is compelled to content itself with explaining the will by a recital of its activities.

The will is elusive. When we think that we have pinned it down for an examination of its essential nature, we find that we have merely laid hold of one of its manifold phases of activity. The will in itself remains free from our confining instruments, defying us to fasten it down even by a satisfactory definition. Compared with the knowledge we have of the fundamental nature of the emotions, the reason, the memory, and the imagination, our knowledge of the essential nature of will is very unsatisfactory. Yet at the same time, we know that we have a will and that we will; and, moreover, we know how to train our will and how to develop and unfold its power.

We have but to attempt to define the will, even with the aid of the best dictionaries, in order to realize how far beyond all possible definitions of it is our intuitive and direct knowledge of its presence, its powers, its activities. Turning to the dictionaries, we find that *will* is defined as: "The power of the mind that enables a person to choose between two courses of action; also, the actual exercise of the power of choice," and, in a secondary meaning, "strong wish or inclination; desire or conative feeling." The dictionaries further inform us that "the power of choice" is the distinctive attribute of will, and the exercise of that power is more properly called "volition."

Now, this definition is not in accord with the fuller conception of the term *will*, which most of us entertain; moreover, it is not in full accord with the teaching of the best modern psychology. Most of us, when we employ the term *will*, have in mind the exercise of the strong, purposeful, determined power of the ego, or "I AM I." We know that within ourselves is a strong dynamic force that, when applied with a set and determined purpose, is capable

THE NATURE OF WILL

of acting with tremendous force, overcoming obstacles, breaking barriers, and sweeping away opposition. Moreover, the best modern psychology informs us that will always is concerned with action, and without action there is no completed process of will.

In the present book, we shall consider will as being essentially concerned with action and as being most characteristically manifested in the mental states we know as "purpose" and "determination," respectively. All the other phases of will we shall regard as being merely incidental to this phase of *purposeful determination,* and as contributing to such phase. By following this course, we shall be emphasizing the practical aspect of willpower and be keeping the inquiry and instruction in the channel promising the greatest benefit to you in the accomplishment of your ends and aims, your ambitions and your hopes.

The term *purpose* seems to express satisfactorily this understanding and conception of will. It is defined as: "The view, aim, design, intention, determination, resolution, or will to accomplish or reach some particular object." Another definition is: "That which a person sets before themselves as the object to be gained or accomplished; the end or aim which one has in view in any plan, measure, or exertion; that which one intends to do, hence their intention, design, plan, or project." Employed as a verb, the term *purpose* is defined as: "To intend, to design, to determine or resolve on anything as an end or object to be gained or accomplished."

The term, *determination*, in this particular meaning, is defined as: "Strength or firmness of mind; firm resolve or resolution; and absolute direction to a certain end."

In the mental state of *purposeful determination* and in its resultant action, we have at least a "working principle" of the phase of willpower with which we are vitally concerned in this book. We shall consider and apply the principles of the other phases of will toward the end of the accomplishment of I "purposeful determination" phase of willpower. We ask you to fix this principle in your mind and to keep it in view throughout the entire course of this inquiry and instruction. Memorize the term *purposeful determination.*I think it well to present at this point a brief and general synopsis of the five stages of will—the stages which each and every process of will manifests as it unfolds into active expression. The more clearly you understand the processes of will, the more clearly will you be able to will. These five stages of will are as follows:

1. Feeling and emotion

2. Desire and impulse

3. Deliberation and consideration

4. Determination and decision

5. Voluntary expression and actionHere follows a brief description of each of the above-stated five stages of will.

1. THE STAGE OF FEELING AND EMOTION

Feeling is defined as: "The simple agreeable or disagreeable side of any mental state." *Emotion* is the complex of feeling. Feeling is the indispensable element of all emotional states. While feeling in itself is not to be regarded as a phase or aspect of perfected will, yet it is true that feeling is one of the "raw materials" of *will action*. Or, stating it in another form, all will-activities have their roots embedded in the soil of feeling and emotion. This fact is not generally recognized by the average person, but it is one that everyone is forced to admit when they analyze and examine their will-processes. In the category of feeling and emotion I, of course, include the moral and religious feelings and emotions, as well as each and every other form of feeling and emotion.

It has well been said, "The phenomena of the world have value to us only in so far as they affect our feelings." The importance of this is recognized when we realize that all will-activities proceed from desire, and that desire is but the active aspect or phase of feeling. We "will" to do only what we desire to do; and we desire to do only what our feelings report as comfortable, satisfying, and contenting, rather than the opposite. If an object fails to arouse interest and agreeable feelings—if it thus possesses no interest or attraction for us—then we experience no desire or impulse to do anything concerning the attainment of that object.

If we have no aversion or repulsion (also phases of feeling) concerning an object, then we experience no desire or impulse to avoid or escape or to get rid of or away from it. Without agreeable or disagreeable feelings or interest concerning any particular thing, we have no desire or impulse to act in any way concerning or relating to that thing—it has no will-value for us in such case.

If feelings and emotions were eliminated from our mental being, then all things alike would prove absolutely uninteresting to us. In such case, in the familiar phrase, all things would "look alike to us"—we should not *want* any of them, nor should we want to take any action toward attaining any of them; likewise, we should not *dislike* any of them nor should we want to take any action in the direction of escaping, avoiding, or getting away from anything whatsoever. In such case, our will would be so absolutely passive and inert that it might as well be non-existent.

2. THE STAGE OF DESIRE AND IMPULSE

The essential active element of desire and impulse is, in psychology, called *conation*, which is defined as: "That element of consciousness which shows itself in tendencies, impulses, desires, and acts of volition; it is essentially a mental state of unrest, and it manifests whenever a mental state tends by its nature to develop into something else."

Desire is defined as: "A conative tendency toward that which promises emotional satisfaction and content, or else away from that which threatens emotional dissatisfaction and discontent." Desire has for its object the satisfaction of some form of pleasurable feeling, or the escape from some form of painful feeling. This pleasurable or painful feeling, however, may be concerned with either *immediate* or *remote* events; likewise, such events may concern either the *individual* or *others* in whom they are interested and to whom they are related by the bonds of affection or sympathy. No matter how complex may be the feelings arousing the conative impulses of desire, their ultimate analysis will show that the basic feeling is that inspired by some promised pleasure or some threatened pain, immediate or remote, direct or indirect, deemed likely to be experienced by the individual.

Desire is the connecting link between feeling and will. On one side it is blended with feeling, on the other side it blends into will. It depends for existence upon feeling; it depends for expression upon will. Desire always manifests by a more or less definite "want" or "want to," accompanied by a peculiar feeling of tension or strain, known as impulse. The stronger the desire, the stronger is this tension or strain of impulse—this conative urge toward action.

Feeling and emotion inspiring desire may manifest on the open plane of consciousness; they may abide more or less concealed in the recesses of the subconscious mentality;

or they may exist in the guise of habit. But wherever they exist or abide, or in whatever form or guise they present themselves, they are always feeling and emotion in the stage of transformation into the conative energy of desire, striving to escape and find release in *voluntary action* of the will.

3. THE STAGE OF DELIBERATION AND CONSIDERATION

Deliberation is: "The act of weighing in the mind." In this stage you find yourself confronted with several alternative courses of action, or else with the question "to do or not to do" some particular thing. In each and every instance of deliberation, however, you will find that each alternative course of action will involve certain phases of desire—certain tendencies to attain or to secure something promising emotional satisfaction and content, or else to escape from and to avoid something threatening emotional dissatisfaction and discontent.

These alternative appeals of desire to will present conflicting emotional attractions or repulsions, or both; these you weigh one against the other—one set against the other—until finally you strike the balance of decision. In such cases, you will find yourself (figuratively speaking) tasting these several dishes of emotional food, noting the agreeable or disagreeable qualities of each, and endeavoring to decide which promises the greater degree of emotional satisfaction or dissatisfaction, content or discontent.

The fact that in this process of deliberation you call upon reason, memory, imagination, and other mental powers or faculties to assist you in your decision must not cause you to overlook the all-important part played in it by desire. You will find that in the end you have decided upon the course of action that promises you the greatest emotional content and comfort and the least emotional dissatisfaction and discomfort. You have employed reason, and its assistant faculties and powers, merely to enable you to discover which of the alternatives possesses the greater promise of ultimate and permanent emotional value along the lines of content and comfort. Your "reasons" governing your decision concerning will-action are always found to be based upon motives of this particular kind.

4. THE STAGE OF DETERMINATION AND DECISION

Determination in this usage is: "The act of terminating or bringing to an end; the state of decision." In this stage, the processes of deliberation, or the "weighing of motives," is brought to an end and "the mind is made up." The old school of psychology held this to be the last and final act of will—its characteristic act. This would be true if we could accept the old definition of will as "the faculty which chooses or makes choice." But under the later conceptions and definitions of will, in which it is perceived that will is essentially concerned with action, we need to pursue our inquiry further.

There is a marked difference between merely "making up your mind" or of even "deciding to act" and the actual performance of the action you have decided to perform. Many a time you have "made up your mind" and have "decided to act," only later to fail to act or to carry out your decision. This distinction is illustrated by William James' familiar story of the man "making up his mind" and deciding to get out of bed on a cold morning when the alarm clock sounded. Frequently he finds it necessary to "make up his mind" and to "decide" several times before he finally expresses the thought in action.

In this book, we recognize a further phase of determination, which is defined as, "Strength and firmness of mind; firm resolve or resolution; absolute direction to a certain end." In this phase of the stage of determination, you reach the process of *purposeful determination*—here the stage of determination blends into that of *voluntary action* and becomes one with it.

5. THE STAGE OF VOLUNTARY EXPRESSION AND ACTION

Voluntary action is defined as: "The process of acting and moving by willpower." This is the final stage of the will. It is will in full flower. It is toward this end that will has been struggling and striving, which has given activity to all of the processes of the preceding stages or phases of will. Voluntary action is the very spirit of will. Without the manifestation of voluntary action, the will process is practically incomplete.

Determination is the decision to will; in its more active phases it is the resolve or resolution, the purposeful determination to will; in still more intense manifestation, it is even the will to will itself. But in voluntary action we have what has been called "will willing itself in action and manifesting itself as will." Here the trigger of the will has been pulled by the "I AM I." Here the spring of action has been released. Here the will drives itself into action—sets itself to work. Here the will not only "wills to will" but also actually "wills" itself into full manifestation and expression. Here we have the real will—will expressing its purpose, its determination, and its full power and inner nature.

This is the phase of will that so eludes our definition and formal terms, because we have no terms, other than those of will itself, with which to define it. In the previous phases or stages we could employ the terms of feeling, desire, or reason in striving to indicate the nature of the processes of such stages or phases; but here we have nothing else with which to compare will—for there is nothing else of its kind. Will is unique, *sui generis*, alone in its class, in a class by itself. You cannot hope to apprehend intellectually its essential nature; but you can and do know it, and experience it within yourself, as the closest instrument, implement, and power of the "I AM I," the ego, the self!

Expression and Inhibition

There are two general phases or forms of voluntary action with which you must become acquainted. The first phase or form is that of *expression*. Here the will-action proceeds in the direction of the actual expression and manifestation of the mental states animating and inspiring the will. The second phase or form is that of *inhibition*. Here the will-action proceeds in the direction of checking, restraining, keeping back, or inhibiting the expression of certain insistent but objectionable mental states seeking to inspire the will to action. Here the effort is exerted in response to the stronger, opposing mental states that have won in the will conflict during the stage of deliberation and decision. In inhibition, the will is employed for the purpose of binding, locking up, and restraining the activity of the defeated set of desires, which repeatedly present themselves in an attempt to reverse the former decision of the will.

Many regard the phase of expression as the characteristic activity of voluntary action, and from one point of view this is correct. But you should never lose sight of the fact that the person who can and will manifest the phase of inhibition, when necessity arises and wisdom dictates such course, is nonetheless the person of giant willpower. In fact, the person of the strong will usually accomplishes their great results of expression only after they have manifested inhibition in the direction of refraining from acting upon many very strong impulses and desires that are opposed to their "top values" of will. In many cases, indeed, a person employs in inhibition a degree of willpower not less than that required in the processes of expression. It often is quite as hard *not to do a thing* as it is to *do a thing.* The person of purposeful determination and willpower achieves distinction very largely by reason of the fact that they are able to hold before their mental vision one ideal or set of ideals—one set of prime motives, one set purpose, one top value—and then resolutely and determinedly, even ruthlessly, to thrust from their region of will all conflicting and opposing tendencies and desires, inclinations and impulses, urges and cravings. In order to manifest into action the one great ideal, such a person finds it necessary to inhibit and to restrain a host of lesser ideas, desires, inclinations, urges, and cravings. In order to accomplish *one great thing*, you will often find it necessary not to do many other things which conflict with and oppose that one great thing.

In the exercises that form a part of this instruction, you will be asked to manifest this phase of inhibition by willpower. By doing so, you will make progress in the attainment of the giant will. Not necessarily because of any special demerit or evil in the inhibited desires and actions, but simply and solely because by reason of such deliberate and determined action of the will you may develop will-muscle, and may learn how to hold fast the fiery steeds of desire that are pulling your chariot of will.

The steeds of desire serve well their rightful purposes when they are held well in hand; unrestrained, they frequently run away and end by overturning the chariot and perhaps destroying the driver. Their training consists of alternative stimulation and inhibition, deliberately and determinedly devised and executed. The purpose of the training is that, through actual practice and exercise, the fiber of your will shall be made strong and firm, tough and tenacious. By training your desire-nature to submit to the control of the will intelligently applied—and by training your will to control intelligently your desire-nature—you not only develop the art of efficient voluntary action but also train the desire-nature to exert to the full its wonderful powers, or else to withhold its forces when the object of the purposeful determination is best served by such restraint.

Expression and inhibition are the two great levers of your machinery of will. Acquire the art of employing each efficiently and effectively, under the guidance and direction of your reason, and in the service of your prime motives, your top values, your great ideals.

CHAPTER 3

CONATIVE WILL

In your task of developing and training your willpower you must carefully acquaint yourself with each and every one of the several stages or phases of will, to the end that you may master each particular phase in turn. In order to acquire complete control over your processes of willing, you must master each of the phases of the general activity involved in them. You must attack the subject in detail, conquering each of the phases or divisions in turn. When you have made this conquest of the several divisions or phases, you will find that you have made a conquest of the whole.

If you have failed heretofore to attain the conquest of willpower, you will probably find that your failure has resulted from the fact that you have made the mistake of attempting a frontal attack upon the opposing army—directing your attack upon its strongest point where it is able to bring to bear upon you the maximum of its defensive strength. Such attempts usually result in defeat. The true general attacks the flanks of the enemy, cutting off his bases of supply, and then defeating him in detail. This method of attack is the plan which in this book I advise you to follow. I will teach you how to gain control of the bases of supplies, and then how to attack one flank after another until you have gained the control and mastery of the entire organized forces of willpower. Having accomplished this, you may then press these captured forces into your own service, causing them to fight for you instead of against you.

You should begin your attack upon that wing of the army of will that may be called the general phase of conative will. In this category we include the feeling and desire phases of will, which have been indicated in the preceding section of this book.

Conation is defined as: "That element of our mental states that shows itself in tendencies, impulses, desires, and acts of volition." Conation essentially is unrest. It exists when and so far as an existing mental state tends by its nature to develop into something else. Conation manifests itself in an attempt, an endeavor, a striving to attain something of which the idea or mental image exists in consciousness or subconsciousness. A typical instance is that effort of the memory to recall a name that has escaped recollection for the moment. It is, on the mental plane, akin to that which on the physical plane is manifested as muscular strain arising from contraction of the muscles, plus a feeling of pleasantness or unpleasantness, as the case may be.

A leading reference work says: "Conation is common to desire, yearning, longing, craving, wishing, and willing; indeed to all states of consciousness that have an inherent tendency to pass beyond themselves. In desire, consciousness endeavors to pass from the want of an object to the possession thereof; or, if an unpleasantly toned idea enters consciousness—say the idea of an embarrassing situation—a conation arises, and consciousness makes a forcible effort to eject the unpleasant idea."

Conation is that mental state in which the feeling element of desire tends to transform itself into the element of will—where it transforms the "I want" or "I want to" into "I do." It follows the rule of desire that causes the movement toward the object or condition promising the greater emotional satisfaction and content, and away from the object or condition threatening the greater emotional dissatisfaction and discontent. Will arises from affection; affection arises from emotion and feeling. Affection says, "I like." Desire says, "I want" or "I want to," and will says, "I do." In order to understand conative will, you must first understand and control the feelings, emotions, and affections from which conative will springs.

Very few people realize that feeling, emotion, affection, and desire are really phases of will. Psychology, however, informs us that the conative will is the supply department of the army of willpower; that it is the branch of the willpower organization that supplies the active branches of the service with the material with which they work and without which they cannot manifest activity. It is very important for you to realize this fact fully, because you must begin your work of developing and training the will by acquiring control over the processes of the feelings, emotions, affections, and desires that go to make up what is called *conative will.*

You are familiar with the praise accorded to the strong will, but very likely you are not quite so familiar with the fact that under the surface of that valuable mental quality and power there must always exist a strong, ardent, insistent, and persistent desire. Without strong, ardent, insistent desire, even the strongest will will fail to be called into action. Well has it been said that "Desire is the flame, the heat of which generates the steam of will." The people of "strong will" are almost always found to be people of strong desire. What is called "aspiration" and "ambition" is really merely a special form of strong desire given definite form and direction by idea. Likewise, all forms of religious or spiritual craving or moral aspirations are forms of desire.

Nearly everyone believes that they have desire well developed within their being, but, as a matter of fact, very few people have even begun to realize just what desire really is. The great masses of people believe desire to be merely the faint, colorless "wanting" or the equally gentle and mild "wishing" that represents the extent of their development of conative will. They usually have not even the most remote idea of what it means or *feels like* to be filled with that eager, longing, craving, ravenous desire that expresses itself in an insistent demand for the desired object or condition—not in a mere "wishing" for it or perhaps even "longing" for it.

Such people have no conception or experience of what it is to *want* a thing as fiercely, insistently, persistently, ardently, overwhelmingly, and vitally as the drowning person wants a breath of air; as the shipwrecked or desert-lost person wants a drink of water; as the famished person wants food; as the fierce, wild creature wants its mate; as the mother wants the welfare of her young. Until they know by actual experience what it feels like to want in this way, they do not know what desire really is. You will note that I repeatedly employ the above illustration of insistent desire in this instruction. I do so purposely, that its repetition will stamp it indelibly upon your mind.

But those individuals of the race who have accomplished great things—those great masters of circumstance, those great directors of fate, along all lines of human life and endeavor—these people know full well what it means to experience this fierce, elemental thirst of desire. Their strong willpower has been aroused into action, and maintained in persistent and determined action, by the elemental force thus set into manifestation and expression.

Such men and women act upon the principle that "You may have anything you want, provided that you want it hard enough," and they begin by *wanting it hard enough.* The failure of many people is originally caused by their lack of the power to want things hard enough. When you learn to want a thing hard enough, you will have taken the second great step on the *path of attainment,* which is mounted by the energy of willpower. The first step is that of knowing just what you want, definite ideals, and insistent desire—these, with will, are the prerequisites of persistent determination.

Desire supplies the motives for all action of the will. Without these motives, the will would not proceed to action at all, in any direction whatsoever. If you had no desire concerning a particular thing, then you would not manifest will-activity toward or away from that particular thing. In such case, you would remain perfectly neutral and passive in your attitude toward that thing. This holds good concerning your mental attitude and action toward or away from anything or everything.

The general rule concerning the effect and influence of desire upon will-activity is as follows: You always act in the direction which, at that particular moment of consciousness, seems to promise the greatest degree of emotional satisfaction and content, or which threatens the least degree of emotional dissatisfaction or discontent—the promise or threat being either direct or indirect, immediate or remote in time and place.

This rule holds good even when you act to relinquish an immediate or present good in favor of a future or remote good; also when you relinquish a present good because of the fear of some unpleasant remote or future consequence of the action. In all cases, you will find that your actions are based upon the rule that a person always seeks that which will bring them pleasure or get rid of pain, immediate or remote, for themselves or for others to whom they are bound by ties of sympathy or affection. This pleasure or pain may be on the planes of physical, mental, moral, or spiritual-emotional feeling, respectively—the principle applies to all planes of emotional activity and manifestation.

The technical rule of psychology concerning will action is as follows: "The will proceeds to action along the lines of the strongest motives present and active, in thought and in feeling, at the moment of the action." In considering this rule, you must always remember that the *motive* always is to be found in feeling, emotion, or affection, raised to the conative plane of desire; this being more or less influenced and directed by reason. Reason, intellect, memory, and imagination, however, serve merely as the directors and aids to the desire element of will in such cases. At the last, they are seen but to serve to point out the road over which the strongest desires may travel most efficiently and successfully, and whereby undesirable consequences may be avoided—they indicate merely the "how" and the direction whereby the desire may be most effectively and fully satisfied.

The realization of this absolute but comparatively little-known rule concerning will action brings us to some startling logical conclusions when we seek to reason out the matter to its end. We then see that our highest and most unselfish, as well as our lowest and most selfish actions are performed under this same rule. You must not for a moment fall into the error of identifying desire with merely the unworthy examples of that mental state; on the contrary, the very highest aims, aspirations, ambitions, and striving toward high ideals are likewise in the category of desire. Anything that we wish to do, want to do, or strive to do—high or low, egoistic or altruistic, moral or immoral, social or unsocial, commendable or reprehensible, material or spiritual—all these are forms of desire based upon feeling, emotion, affection. The highest morality is that based upon the strong feeling, emotion, affection, and desire to live a moral life, which satisfies and contents the spirit, rather than upon fear, or the mere wish to be well-regarded by other people and to meet with popular approval.

But here, you must not fall into the error or fallacy of believing that humans are mere automatons moved hither and thither by desire, or mere helpless slaves of desire. While it is true that you act by and through your will and that desire is the *motive* of will-activity, it likewise is true that by the introduction of ideas and ideals even desire is given form and direction—strength and power toward a definite end. By means of the scientific introduction of ideas and ideals, you may give to any form, phase, aspect, or mode of desire and feeling a degree of strength and power that it did not possess previously.

In such cases, your will wills that desire shall be in accordance with will; it wills that it shall be supplied with the right kind of desire power which is required in order to call into activity the needed degree of willpower. The untrained will is like a stream flowing through a channel dug for it by others; the trained will, on the contrary, first digs its own channel and then flows through its self-imposed, self-limited banks and walls—it is self-limited, and, at the last, self-directed.

Keen reasoners, at this point, sometimes object that even in such cases will is moved by desire in some form or degree. Such reasoners hold that all that the will accomplishes in such cases is to master one set of feelings and desires in favor of a higher and more dominant set. This is close reasoning; it is logically correct and has never been successfully controverted. But, even so, the principle of the control of desire by the will remains undisturbed, so far as concerns its pragmatic and practical application.

While you may never expect to escape the influence of desire, even in your highest will-activities, yet you may stand upon the high position of the dominant will, and from that position may control, stimulate, weaken, encourage, or depress the power of the lower forms of desire and feeling. In fact, when you reach the heights of willpower, you will find that the element of desire seems almost to blend into the essential element of will itself—almost to become identical with it. In such cases, you will be forced to the conscious conviction that here, at the last, you have ceased merely to *desire to will* and instead have reached the point where you are able to *will to will.*Be the metaphysical theory whatever it may, the fact remains that to the person who has climbed the heights of will there sooner or later comes this supreme report of consciousness of the freedom of the ultimate will. But such heights are reached only by those individuals who have paid the price of attainment—who have persistently climbed the steep mountain paths of willpower and have at last reached the clear space at the top. Such experiences are unknown to the great masses of people. The average person is practically the slave of desire—usually of their cruder and most primitive ones. They do not understand even the first principles of the mastery of desire by the dominant will. The great mass of people are *will slaves*—there are but few real *will masters.*

Here, in a nutshell, is the distinction between the will slave and the will master: The average person is moved to will-activity by the forces of feeling, affection, and desire—the strongest desire-motive always winning the day. Those who have arrived at a scientific understanding of the subject, however, know that while it is true that the strongest desire always wins the battle, nevertheless, it is equally true that the strength of feeling, affection, and desire is directly proportionate to the strength of the ideas or ideals animating it. Consequently, by the skillful employment of attention (itself one of the principal weapons of will) in the direction of holding in consciousness a certain set of ideas or ideals, one may cause these ideas or ideals to energize the set of feelings and desires associated with them, and at the same time to weaken the opposite set of feelings and desires.

By the control of the attention, the "I AM I," through the will, is able to control feeling and desire, to make them act as his servants, and thus to attain to the mastery of will. By the scientific employment of ideas and ideals, through the attention, you may control, direct, and master the activities of the conative will. But, as we have said, the average person has not even the faintest glimmering of this truth—and, as a consequence, such person remains throughout their life a will slave instead of becoming a will master.

It is an axiom of psychology that: "The degree of force, energy, will, determination, persistence, and continuous application manifested by an individual in their aspirations, ambitions, aims, performances, actions, and work is determined primarily by the degree of their desire for the attainment of their objects—their degree of 'want' and 'want to' concerning those objects." This is the more technical statement of the principle embodied in the aphorism that has been previously quoted to you: "Desire is the flame that produces the steam of will." The logical inference is that when you wish to produce and use the steam of will you must first supply the full flame of desire.

In my book entitled *Desire Power*, I have considered in close detail the subject of desire in its relation to other forms and phases of personal power, including the phase of willpower. In it I have drawn upon familiar human experiences and upon the facts of natural history concerning animal life, for the purpose of illustrating the nature and character of desire regarded as the motive power of will-activity, etc. The following paragraph, reproduced from the pages of that book, follows the presentation of those illustrations. I advise you to study carefully the principle announced therein and to commit to memory the spirit of those principles, as expressed in the *master formula of attainment*: "You may have anything you want, provided that you 1) know exactly what you want; 2) want it hard enough; 3) confidently expect to obtain it; 4) persistently determine to obtain it; and 5) are willing to pay the price of its attainment."

> I have called your attention to the above examples and illustrations of the force of strongly aroused elemental emotions and desires, not alone to point out to you how strong such feelings, emotions, and desires become under the appropriate circumstances and conditions, but also to bring you to a realization of the existence within all living things of a latent emotional strength and power that is capable of being aroused into strenuous activity under the proper stimulus and directed toward certain definite ends and purposes indicated by that stimulus. That this strength and

power is aroused by, and flows out toward, the particular forms of stimulus above indicated is a matter of common knowledge. But that it may be aroused to equal strength, power, and intensity by other forms of stimulus (such stimulus having been deliberately placed before it by the individual) is not known to the many; only the few have learned this secret. The method whereby the latent desire power may be stimulated by inciting ideas and mental pictures is based upon the following psychological principle: "Desire is aroused by and flows forth toward things represented by suggestive ideas and mental pictures; the stronger and clearer the suggestive idea or mental picture, the stronger and more insistent is the aroused desire, all else being equal." Knowing and applying this principle renders you the master of desire instead of the slave of desire.

The following quotation from Professor Halleck will serve to illustrate the principle involved in the process of employing the power of attention in presenting to desire the stimulus of suggestive ideas and mental images in order to more fully arouse and to further strengthen the feeling and conative tendency. Halleck says: The first step in the development of the will lies in the exercise of attention. There is a sense of effort in voluntary attention.

Ideas grow in distinctness and in motor power as we attend to them. If we take two ideas of the same intensity and center the attention upon one, we shall notice how much it grows in power. Take the sensations from two aches in the body and fix attention upon those of one of them. That idea will grow in motor power until we may act in a direction supposed to relieve that special pain, while the other is comparatively neglected. If we, at the start, want several things in about an equal degree, whether a bicycle, a typewriter, or an encyclopedia, we shall end by wanting that the most on which our attention has been most strongly centered. The bicycle idea may thus gain more motor power than either of the two other; or, if we keep thinking how useful a cyclopedia would be, action may tend in that direction.

We may state as a law the fact that the will determines which motive shall become the strongest, by determining which ideas shall occupy the field of consciousness.

Every idea which becomes an object of desire is a motive. It is true that the will tends to go out in the direction of the greatest motive, that is, toward the object which seems most desirable; but the will, through voluntary attention, puts energy into a motive idea and thus makes it strong. It is impossible to center the attention long upon an idea, without developing positive or negative interest (attraction or repulsion). Thus does the will develop motives. We have seen that emotion and desire arise in the presence of ideas, and that the will has influence in detaining or banishing a given idea. If one idea is kept before the mind, a desire and strong motive may gather around that idea. If another idea is called in, the power of the first will decline. The more Macbeth and his wife held before themselves the idea of the fame and power which the throne would confer upon them, the stronger became the desire to kill the king, until it finally grew too strong to be mastered. They were, however, responsible for nursing the desire; had they resolutely thought of something else, the desire would have been weakened. The "suggestive ideas and mental pictures" that I have urged you to employ in order to arouse and heighten the vigor and power of desire are as follows: suggestive ideas and mental pictures serving to awaken deeper and stronger feelings and emotions concerning the object of your desire, and tending toward awakening a stronger degree of affection for that object, which, as a consequence, heightens the flame of desire and thus produces a greater pressure of the steam of will. These suggestive ideas and mental pictures should "tempt the appetite" of the desire by presenting to it pictures and suggestions of the satisfaction and content, pleasure and joy that will follow the achievement or attainment of the objects of the desire.

This principle is elaborated in my book entitled *Desire Power*, in which are also given suggestions and methods designed to aid the working out of the principle.

CHAPTER 4

DELIBERATIVE
WILL

You are now asked to consider the phase of willpower known as the stage of deliberative will. *Deliberation* is defined as, "The act of weighing in the mind." In the stage of deliberation you weigh with more or less care the courses of action presenting themselves to the will. Each of the alternative courses possesses certain points of attraction and also certain points of repulsion.

The attractive points arise from the promise of emotional satisfaction and content; the points of repulsion arise from the threat of emotional dissatisfaction and discontent. These opposing points are to be balanced one against the other, to the end that the stage of determination and the resulting stage of voluntary action may be reached and the processes of will thereby completed.

You probably have been accustomed to regard the process of deliberation as one concerned solely with intellectual activity. You probably have imagined that when you deliberate concerning alternative courses of action, you approach the matter in the spirit of cold reasoning, and your decision is made wholly from the standpoint of logical judgment. But, as a matter of fact, the part played by your intellect and reason in deliberating action, and in the judgments resulting from this, usually is merely the part of the searcher after facts relating to 1) the direction and means whereby the greatest emotional satisfaction and content may be secured; and 2) the probable results of the action along the lines of either of the two alternative courses—those results always being measured by their probable effect upon your state of emotional satisfaction and content.

In short, your reason is employed to search the records of experience in order to discover the associations and relations of each of the two alternative courses of action, to the end that you may have the fullest possible information concerning the probable ultimate emotional value of each action; and also to discover and recommend to the will the most effective methods whereby you may apply either course of action.

It is true that in people of trained intellectual powers, wide experience, well-stocked memory, and active constructive imagination, the intellectual faculties play a far more important part in the processes of deliberation and decision than in people lacking those mental qualifications and this extended experience.

Reason performs valuable services by holding up to the will the probable results of various courses of action so that the will may more clearly determine the actual emotional value of those courses. It also renders valuable service to the will in the matter of discovering, uncovering, inventing, and creating methods whereby the "good" of the will may best be realized and expressed. In this and in similar ways, it provides the will with positive and negative motives for choice and action, and thus throws additional weight into the alternative courses being deliberated.

Reason serves will in this way by placing its forces of memory, imagination, and association of ideas at the disposal of will. It also aids will by furnishing it with the fullest possible information concerning the alternative courses of action under consideration—by "telling it all about them" to the best of its ability. This is of the greatest value in the process of deliberation, and very often determines the decision.

A course of action "clearly and definitely known" has a very great advantage as a candidate for will-action over one not so known. Reason proceeds to aid will in this way with a machine-like coldness, provided that emotion be kept from interfering with the work. Reason has nothing to gain but the satisfaction of its own nature in thought.

Reason is very cold-blooded and tends to proceed with the appalling inexorableness of a machine. It is unfeeling and unmoral—it proceeds logically from premise to conclusion without regard to emotional or moral values.

But at the last, reason acting as an aid to will always operates merely in discovering the facts of the probable emotional value of courses of action under consideration. Otherwise, reason plans and decides upon the most effective methods of expressing and manifesting those desires, ideas, and ideals connected that have been accepted by the will as containing the promise of emotional value. In short, reason in such cases is concerned merely with the task of uncovering certain courses of action possessing emotional value. This emotional value is always determined by the greater degree of promised emotional satisfaction and content or the least degree of threatened emotional dissatisfaction and discontent.

You should note here, however, the following distinction: The emotional element is directly involved only in deliberation and decision concerning the advisability of performing certain actions or courses of action. It is involved in this way in all questions of "to do or not to do" and all questions of "which of these two courses of action shall I choose?" It is not involved in this way in cases of purely intellectual effort or processes of logical reasoning, as, for instance, in the working out of problems of formal logic or mathematics. Neither is it directly involved in cases in which reason is called upon to decide and determine which of certain ideas, plans, methods, or courses of procedure will best serve to accomplish certain definite ends and aims. In cases of the latter class, the deliberation and decision concerning the advisability of undertaking certain tasks, or courses of action, has been previously performed along the lines of comparative emotional value; all that now remains to be deliberated and decided is *how* best to carry out and execute the designs already adopted, and in what way may best be accomplished the ends already accepted as being emotionally advantageous.

The rule, however, applies invariably to all cases in which you experience the conflicting pulls or pushes of "In one way I want to do this, while in another way I do not want to do it"; or in cases in which you say to yourself, "This seems to be what I want, or to lead to what I want; but I fear that it may bring about complications I do not want"; or where you say to yourself, "I want to do this, and I want to do that; but I do not know which I want to do more than the other." In such cases the conflict really is a desire conflict, or an emotional conflict, and not a direct intellectual conflict at all.

You may feel inclined to resent this statement, and probably may even indignantly deny its truth—many people feel this way when first this fact is presented to them. Most of us like to think that we decide every question of conduct and action from the standpoint of pure logic and cold reason, but we do not do so at all in cases, such as I have just mentioned. If you cannot see the truth of this statement and are inclined to dispute it, you would do well to submit it to the following test of your own reason and experience and settle it at once and for all. Unless it is settled in your mind, you may not be able to enter fully into the spirit of certain points of our instruction, which are based upon this particular psychological principle.

Here is the test of reason and experience. Apply it to yourself, honestly and in the scientific spirit, and answer it in the same way. Ask yourself the following questions:

- "What are the true reasons governing my decisions concerning taking courses of action and conduct or refraining from them, in which the element of feeling, emotion, affection, or desire is involved?"

- "Do I or do I not consider and decide the question of 'shall I or shall I not' or 'which shall I do or choose?' from the standpoint of securing the greatest emotional satisfaction and content or the least emotional dissatisfaction and discontent—the greatest pleasure or the least pain?"

In answering these questions, you should bear in mind that the pleasure and pain may be immediate or remote, and may be concerned directly with your own personal experience or that of others to whom you are connected by the bonds of sympathy or affection. All of these forms of emotional satisfaction and content, or emotional dissatisfaction and discontent, come under the general rule.

A careful self-analysis and a frank, honest report based thereupon is certain to bring to you the conviction that your deliberations and decisions concerning your actions or courses of conduct invariably are made upon this basis of the greatest emotional value. The "reasons" for your actions are never divorced from your feelings, affections, and desires. In fact, in the absence of feeling, affection, and desire there could not and would not be any "reasons" at all for your actions or courses of conduct. The only reason— the only *cause* and *because*—of your actions, your choice of actions, or of your acting at all is the reason, the *cause*, and the *because* arising from the promise of emotional satisfaction and content, or the threat of the opposite results—the probable emotional value, in short, passed upon to some extent by reason.

Sometimes it is difficult to trace back the path to the determining feeling, affection, or desire of an action or course of conduct, so remote or so complex it may be at times. But the influence of the feeling, the affection, or the desire is always there, animating and inspiring the action or course of conduct. Otherwise, there would and could be no reason, cause, or because at all for your conduct or action, and, consequently, no answer to the question "why" concerning such action or conduct. In this connection you should remember that I include *habit* among the emotional motives—you know that it is more comfortable to act according to habit than contrary thereto, and "comfortable" implies feeling and desire.

Before conative will is transformed into active will there must be mental activity in the stage of deliberation. Conative will becomes transformed into active will only in response to some idea or object calling it forth into expression and manifestation. There are usually several alternative ideas or objects presented to the will for decision and choice—or at least there is the alternative of "to do or not to do." Here, deliberative will, assisted by intellect, weighs and appraises these conflicting alternatives. The process of deliberation may be extended over a considerable period of time, or else it may be almost instantaneous—but it is always performed.

Pleasure and pain, agreeable or disagreeable mental states, are the precedents of all definite activities of will. Action is found always to proceed toward the most agreeable and away from the most disagreeable mental state. The will is always interested—never disinterested—in its actions. It always moves to gain some end—to acquire something that to it seems "good."

Life is largely a matter of securing the agreeable and escaping the disagreeable. But it must not be forgotten that by shifting the mental point of view our emotional feelings often change from the agreeable to the disagreeable and vice versa. Sometimes there is a violent shifting from one pole to the other of our emotional nature. Such changes arise from the discovery of new attributes in the objects and ideas presenting themselves for deliberation, decision, and determination. Thus, while feeling, affection, and desire are the motives for all will actions, the other mental faculties play an important part by presenting to them the ideas and mental images that tend to influence and direct the emotional faculties and thus have an important influence on will itself.

FINDING YOUR DEFINITE PURPOSES

I shall now illustrate the process of deliberative will by an appeal to your own personal experience. While doing this, you will also be obtaining some practical exercise along the lines of efficient deliberative will work and activity. In the following illustrations and examples, you will take several important steps in the direction of actual practice and training of your willpower. Instead of illustrating the principles in question by introducing abstract and impersonal examples or instances, I shall employ illustrations and examples from your own personal experiences, so that in examining these illustrative examples you will at the same time be actually exercising the mental faculties that furnish them.

Begin by asking yourself the following questions:"For what purpose do I wish to develop and train my willpower and to manifest it in action?"

- "In what direction do I wish to apply and employ it when I have acquired it?"

- "What is the chief end that I seek to accomplish and to attain through the possession and manifestation of developed and trained willpower?"

The character of the special instruction and information you obtain from the study of this book depends upon your answers to these questions. Think well over these questions—ponder them carefully and answer them fully, frankly, and honestly to yourself. You will do well to commit your answers to writing for future reference; to "think with pencil and paper" is a very helpful method and one I advise in this course. The following suggestions and advice should materially aid you in this task of discovering and uncovering your definite purposes for which you seek to develop and train your willpower.

If you are like most people who undertake to determine their definite purposes, which they seek to achieve by means of their willpower, you will find yourself perplexed to fully and correctly answer the questions above. You, like many others, probably have not yet "found yourself" in this important matter. That is to say, you have not yet discovered your definite purposes in life. If this is so, then this book has reached you at the right time, because, until you discover your definite purposes, you cannot expect to efficiently employ even the degree of willpower you have already developed, not to speak of the additional degree you hope to attain.

Most people in this stage (and this probably includes yourself) find themselves filled with merely a vague and general—though perhaps quite strong—inclination and tendency to push forward into action to achieve whatever will be "good" for them. They feel the general outward pressure of conative will, but they do not as yet know in just what direction to exert that inner power. This condition is all right so far as it goes—but it does not go far enough. The sense of willpower is there, but willpower without definite purpose is inefficient and useless. There is needed here a strong, definite, positive, purposive direction for the conative will. I shall now present to you the methods that supply this needed element.

DOMINANT DESIRES

In the first place, you should discover your dominant desires—the strongest and most insistent desires that abide within your mental and emotional being. It is no easy matter to discover your dominant desires without some instruction concerning the process. You will find that your mental and emotional being is filled with a multitude of desires—great and small, transient and permanent—many of which oppose and interfere with others. You need to carefully weigh and measure your desires, taking into the calculation the element of depth and width as well as of weight. You must weed the desire garden, cutting away the dead wood of the tree of desire. This is a test of strength and vitality between opposing sets of desires, resulting in the survival of the fittest.

In my book entitled *Desire Power*, I have gone into detail and into an extended consideration of the process of discovering the dominant desires. I refer you to that book if you are especially interested in this subject. I cannot repeat everything in this book. The following condensed synopsis, however, will serve to give you the essence of the general principle involved:

1. The Regions of the Mind

The regions of the mind are explored for the purpose of bringing to light the various feelings, emotions, affections, longings, and desires that compose your emotional nature. These, as they are brought to light, are carefully noted on a written list.

2. *The Process of Elimination*

Then begins the process of elimination as follows: 1) the weaker and less insistent desires, and those plainly of a transient, passing nature, are struck from the list, leaving there only the stronger and more permanent ones; 2) the list is then again carefully scrutinized—those desires that "stand out" by reason of their superior power are retained, the remainder are eliminated; 3) the process is continued along these lines of critical selection until further elimination is deemed inadvisable for fear of "cutting away live wood."

3. *Classification*

Then the surviving desires are arranged into classes, and these classes are subjected to competition with each other, the stronger and more permanent being retained, while the weaker and less permanent are discarded.

4. *Comparison*

Then the surviving sets of desires are compared carefully for the purpose of discovering antagonism and opposition—the qualities of contradiction that render coordination and harmonious cooperation impossible, and which tend to pull the will in two opposite directions and thus to bring it to a standstill.

5. Competition

The opposing and contradictory sets of qualities must be pitted in competition against each other, for one or the other must be discarded from the field of the will. Each must be viewed from every possible mental and emotional angle and subjected to the most rigid tests. The final result will reveal the stronger of each opposing and contradictory sets of qualities—those which have won in "the struggle for existence" and which represent the "survival of the fittest."

The survivors in this process of selection and elimination will represent the strongest and most deeply rooted desires of the individual and will constitute their dominant desires. These dominant desires represent your strongest and most enduring affections, based upon your most vigorous, hardy, and sturdy feelings, and rising to the stage of conative will in the form of insistent desire. They represent that which you "want hard enough"—want so insistently as to render you willing to "pay the price of its attainment."

ENERGIZING IDEAS

But desire is not the only element involved in deliberative will. In fact, it may be said that every great department of mental activity is involved therein. The presence of ideas and ideals is necessary in the process of deliberation.

Action is influenced by representative ideas of objects and things of the outside world. Each clear and strong idea opens a path to possible action, and, therefore, constitutes an element of the deliberative process. Memory and imagination are also called into play with great effect in the processes of deliberative will.

Professor Halleck says:

> The greater variety of ideas a man has, the more numerous are the courses of action open to him. If an intelligent physician has an idea of twenty-five different methods of treating rheumatism, he may vary his treatment accordingly, and may succeed where a less skilled doctor would fail. If a businessperson has a dozen ideas to fit a given emergency, he may act in any one of these directions; if he has but one idea, he can act but in one direction. Idea must proceed to open a path for intelligent action. Before Columbus sailed, he had an idea of land beyond the seas. Even a plumber must have an idea of how to make a short cut for his pipe, before he can do it. The same well-known teacher said:
>
> Deliberation is a process of both intellect and will; of intellect to represent ideas and compare them, and of will to hold the ideas before the attention or to dismiss them and make room for others. In

the deliberative process, the whole person makes themselves felt; all their past experiences count. In impulsive action, the momentary state triumphs.

Let us take a rational human action and see how much deliberation may be involved in it. I wish to leave the city during the heated term. Before I act, I not only have the desire to go, but I must know where to go. I find out the location, the merits, and the defects of a number of summer resorts. Then I proceed to deliberate. A has surf bathing; B is on a mountain and has fine tonic air; C is nearby and some of my friends are going there, but the mosquitoes are annoying and will not allow one to take a walk with any comfort; D has fine air and no mosquitoes, but the place is too fashionable and too much given to dress; E suits for all reasons, save that it is too expensive: F would answer but it is too far off. I then take into my deliberations the possibility of staying all summer in the city. Three hot days come. The nights are so warm that one cannot sleep. I then continue my deliberations about the summer resorts. Will is necessarily present in its most important aspect in every act of deliberation. I balance one idea against another. By willpower I turn my attention undivided upon one idea; then I dismiss it, and turn my attention to another. I consider the surf bathing of A, the mountain air of B, the annoyance at C, the fashion at D, the expense at E, the distance to F. The intellectual faculties are called into play in the processes of deliberative will in the above illustration concerning summer resorts. Deliberative will produces from the region of imagination and memory many facts bearing upon each of the courses of action. It brings up the related facts that add to or detract from the merits of each alternative. It also serves to expose the false nature of some of the courses of action and to add to the validity of others. It acts in the direction of choosing and adapting means to given ends, and it establishes the logical relation of cause and effect between different things. Before you can "know what you want," you must understand the true nature of the alternative wants—you must know the relations and consequences, the associations and the results of particular courses of action.

The person who wishes to know intelligently "just what they want"—and just what course of general action will bring to them the greatest ultimate content and satisfaction—must employ their reasoning faculties in addition to exploring their emotional nature. They must use head as well as heart. They must learn how to observe and examine things, how to obtain correct perceptions, how to form logical judgments, how to use their powers of imagination and memory in the task. As Halleck has said: "In the deliberative process, the whole man makes himself felt."

The subject of deliberative will blends into and harmonizes with that of determinative will in many particulars. Determination is the final step or stage of deliberation and, at the same time, the first step or stage of voluntary action. With this fact in mind, let us now proceed to consider determinative will in the following section.

CHAPTER 5

DETERMINATIVE
WILL

The stage of determination is the fourth stage of the will-process. *Determination* is defined as follows: "1) the act of terminating or bringing to an end; the state of decision; also 2) strength and firmness of mind; firm resolve or resolution and absolute direction to a certain end."

The first definition indicates the termination or ending of the process of deliberation—the decision resulting from the process of deliberation. The second definition indicates the beginning of a new process—the process of impulsion toward voluntary action, and the direction of that impulse. In the following consideration of determinative will, you will see that both of these stages are manifested by will passing through the stage of determination.

You must remember, here, that in studying this subject you are employing a method that may be stated as "finding your definite purposes" and which is represented by the effort to answer the following questions that you have propounded to yourself:

- "For what purpose do I wish to develop and train my willpower and to manifest it in action?"

- "In what direction do I wish to apply and employ it when I have acquired it?"

- "What is the chief end I seek to accomplish and to attain through the possession of developed and trained willpower?"

You have subjected these questions to the test of the deliberative will and are now presenting them to the determinative will for decision and for subsequent positive action upon that decision. The process of deliberation cannot be arrived at without sufficient evidence to warrant an intelligent conclusion.

Professor Halleck illustrates the act of decision following his deliberation concerning the summer resort (previously quoted) as follows:

> With reference to the summer resort, deliberation does not end the voluntary process; the act of will

is yet incomplete. Something more is necessary than 1) a desire to go, and 2) deliberation about a large number of resorts. My next voluntary step is to choose among the many resorts concerning which I have been deliberating, and to decide to go to one. G satisfies my reason, for the place has sailing and fishing, good walks, few mosquitoes, and moderate charges. I then cut short the deliberation and decide to go to G. Decision is a termination of the process of deliberation. The illustration just quoted, however, ends with the performance of the first stage or phase of determinative will—the stage in which the deliberation is brought to an end and the decision made; here the individual says: "I have decided to go to G; I shall go to G." He has "made up his mind" to go to G—but he has not as yet actually set into operation the will-machinery of action upon that decision. He must also come to the point where he can and will truthfully say: "I have now the definite purpose of going to G; I intend to go there, and I now begin to exert my willpower to that end." This last represents the second phase or stage of determinative will.

In considering this particular phase of the activity of the will, we find typical examples of the distinction between the strong, healthy will on the one hand and the weak, flabby will on the other hand. The individuals composing the first class make up their minds firmly and positively and then release their impulsive and directive powers toward the related will-action. The individuals composing the second class, on the contrary, find it most difficult 1) to make up their minds; 2) to keep their minds made up; and 3) to exert their impulsive and directive powers into manifestation and action.

The decision that terminates the process of deliberation is distinctly an act of will, and the sense of voluntary strain and effort is clearly perceptible in the process. Many find decision to be the hardest part of the whole voluntary process. Such people frequently find it almost impossible to make up their minds—to decide and determine their course of action. They have a decided tendency to allow others to make up their minds for them.

Another large class is composed of people who are in the habit of making up their minds in a flash, without due deliberation or exercise of judgment; such people frequently find themselves in trouble as the result of their hasty judgments, and often are required to expend considerable time and energy in their endeavors to rectify matters or to escape from the consequences of their ill-considered decisions. The course of the wise person lies in escaping these two undesirable extremes and in maintaining the Golden Mean between them.

Many people who recognize in themselves the tendency to waver in making decisions, and to escape so far as possible the real act of decision and determination, have vainly sought the cure for their trouble in the conventional advice concerning the use of the will. These people have felt intuitively that there must be some scientific method, based upon sound psychological principles, which would enable them to overcome their handicap and serve to establish a new habit of making decisions and determinations.

Such intuition is well grounded in fact, for such a method does exist and will accomplish its object. In the following several pages, I shall present it to your attention.

In most cases in which it is difficult to arrive at a decision after deliberation, the trouble lies in the fact that the emotional and intellectual values of the conflicting alternatives are too nearly alike to admit of an easy decision.

When the full emotional-intellectual value of the alternatives is clearly perceived, then the decision is easy in most cases, for the weight is clearly on one side. In most cases the choice is made almost automatically. It is axiomatic that the choice between alternatives is quick and easy when their respective values are clearly and definitely known.

In some cases, however, even the process of careful deliberation fails to reveal a preponderance of weight on either side; and the discovery of new attributes has served merely to raise both of the alternative courses to a higher plane of interest, without bestowing upon either a greater proportionate weight. In such cases, the person is like the donkey who starved to death because he was unable to decide between two equally attractive haystacks. It is clear that, if determination is to be reached in such cases, some new element must be introduced.

THE ELEMENT OF FIXED STANDARD

This new element in the task of determination is known as "the element of fixed standard." I ask you to consider carefully the following method designed to apply this added element, for it contains the secret to correct many weaknesses of the will and the key to cultivate prompt, positive, and certain decision and determination.

The essential principle of the fixed standard is: You must establish in your mind a clearly defined, certain, and positive fixed standard of will values based upon an accepted general idea of your *summum bonum*, or chief good, with relative degrees of "goodness" or "badness" on the scale of will values. Those relative degrees are determined by the respective nearness or remoteness to the *summum bonum* or chief good.

This *summum bonum*, or chief good, which constitutes your fixed standard, must be decided upon by yourself— no one else can do the work for you. It must represent your sovereign ideal—your highest conception of general conduct and action—by means of which all special conduct or action is to be measured, weighed, or gauged. The term *standard* is defined as: "That which is established by author-ity as a rule for the measure of quantity, quality, extent, or value; that which is established as a rule or model; a crite-rion; a test." In the present case, your fixed standard is the accepted test, rule, or measure of will value.

Your fixed standard may be modeled upon the character of some great person whom you wish to adopt as a model or, perhaps, upon a composite character made up of the approved and esteemed characteristics of a number of such individuals. Or, again, it may be the idea of some accepted adage, aphorism, or rule of conduct that seems to embody your ideal of behavior and action. For instance, the touch-stone of positivity frequently referred to in our instruction is expressed in the test question: "Will this make me stron-ger, better, and more efficient?"

Or, again, it may be some accepted statement of the gen-eral principle of ethical conduct and action, as, for instance, the celebrated categorical imperative of Kant: "Act always so that you might wish your action and conduct to become the standard of the action of and conduct of all people." Other aphorisms of this kind are the Golden Rule: "Do unto others as you would have others do unto you," or the axiom of Grotius: "Wrong no man, and render unto every man his due."

Or, again, you may adopt as your standard the maxim: "My every action must contribute to my ultimate success"; or the rule that your every action must be in the direction of the betterment of the world, or along the lines of some particular ethical, moral, or religious teachings.

I have mentioned the above examples and illustrations merely to indicate to you the general principle involved, not because you must adopt any one of them. You may have some fixed standard of your own that will far better suit your particular purposes. My purpose here is merely to have you adopt some fixed standard, not any particular one.

However, the *touchstone of positivity*, so frequently mentioned in this book, may be adopted as a sound, practical basis of conduct and action. Rightly interpreted and understood, it represents a very high ideal of practical philosophy. Its test question: "Will this make me stronger, better, and more efficient?" is based upon the threefold ideal of strength, virtue, and efficiency. Surely, that is not an unworthy ideal, and not contrary to the categorical imperative or to the Golden Rule. It could not be objected to as a rule of universal conduct and action or of justice to others. I offer it as a suggestion, but you are free to reject it in favor of a rule of your own, without impairing in any way whatever the application of the principle or the method now to be explained.

Your fixed standard will give you something with which to measure, weigh, or value any and all alternatives of action that are perplexing your determinative will. From it you will build a scale or *table of will values*—a clearly defined and certain scale with which to measure, weigh, and value the courses of action that are constantly presenting themselves for the decision of determinative will. This scale or table of will values must be established as far as possible before the time of actual choice or decision. It must cover so far as is possible every probable demand upon you for decision—particularly the general principle of choice involved in any special subject likely to come prominently before you.

In other words, you must proceed to conduct your deliberation long before the time when your course of action is likely to arrive, so that when the hour of trial comes you will have your basis of decision and determination already firmly and positively made, and thus be able to announce it without delay, backed by the weight of your previous careful consideration. In this way, you really map out or chart in advance the course over which your will shall proceed on its future journeys, and thus you escape the danger of the rocks and reefs that wreck the craft of the mariner lacking such a chart.

In your table of will values you must have numerous degrees or grades of values. At the head of your list must appear your "top values"—certain principles of action of surpassing value to you, which must always be dominant. These top values represent conduct and actions operating to secure results strongly in line with your fixed standard. Thus, if you have adopted the touchstone of positivity, your top values will represent actions and conduct that clearly and positively tend to make you "stronger, better, and more efficient."

Your top values (whatever they may represent) must never be sacrificed, no matter the temptation. Any course of action that contradicts or negates your top values must be rejected at once. Your top values must have an almost religious significance; you must be so inspired by them that a suggestion of their violation will cause you to become horrified and indignant. These top values must be regarded as something sacred and to be treated with reverence.

At the other extreme of the scale there must be "bottom values"—certain courses of action that must be viewed with loathing and disgust and which under no circumstances whatsoever must be followed by you. You must firmly establish these bottom values and keep away from the courses of action and conduct represented by them. There must be no flirting with them, no compromise with them—they must be regarded always as essentially evil and opposed to your real wellbeing and to your permanent happiness, satisfaction, and content. These bottom values must be to you what the Devil was to the old-time orthodox church people—there must be no compromise with Satan; you must always assume the attitude of "Get thee behind me, Satan!" to these bottom values. In case your fixed standard is the touchstone of positivity, then your bottom values will represent those courses of action and conduct that unquestionably make you "weaker, worse, and less efficient."

Between these ever-to-be-sought top values and the ever-to-be-avoided bottom values, there will be a wide range of middle values or neutral values, arranged in their respective places according to their respective degrees of likeness and unlikeness, nearness and remoteness to the values situated at the two respective poles of the scale. Your judgment will dictate the proper place on the scale for each and every kind of value, and you will find it a very interesting task to place and arrange these possible courses of conduct and action upon your scale. You will do well to use pencil and paper here and actually to construct a black and white scale or diagram of this kind.

The main fact to be remembered—the one vital fact upon which the value of the whole system depends—is that the arrangement must be committed to memory so that it may be recalled easily at any time. Each grade, class, or sub-class on the scale must have its own definite and particular place so that it may always be found when looked for; and each class must be definitely set off and apart from the one above it and the one below it on the scale. The more definite and positive your classification, the more effective your scale.

The ideal scale lets you immediately determine which of any two courses of action possesses the greater will value for you. The nearer to this ideal you can come, the more effective will become your table of will values. A little active use of your imagination at this point will convince you of the wonderful service that a table of this kind will render to you. Think of being able to have a table of will values as all-inclusive and as infallible as is the multiplication table! You will find that it is as great an improvement upon the ordinary hit-or-miss method as the use of the multiplication table is an improvement upon "counting off" on your fingers.

If you have gone properly about the work of building your table of will values, you will find that in the end your top values will represent 1) your strongest feelings, emotions, affections, and desires; 2) subjected to the careful scrutiny, analysis, synthesis, and final judgment of your reasoning faculties; and 3) tested by your highest ethical or moral principles and standards. In establishing your table of will values, your physical, mental, moral, and spiritual natures have participated—it represents the essence of your whole nature and character.

When you find yourself confronted with two or more perplexing alternatives calling for decision and determination, you have but to apply to each of the alternatives the following test questions: What place does this proposed course have on my table of will values? How closely does it resemble, harmonize with, and conform to my top values? How far is it away from my bottom values? The answer will give the proper value to you of each of the two alternatives, immediately and directly; your decision and determination will speedily follow. Moreover, by this method the will is trained into the habit of decision and determination along the lines of the highest will values.

However, you must remember that your table of will values may be added to, improved, modified, and subjected to the process of evolutionary development as your experience broadens and widens your intellectual, emotional, and moral horizon. The table of will values of the young person, while properly employed at the time, cannot properly govern the person of matured experience. As with everything else in nature, the law of evolution should govern this table of will values. The system is no rigid, inflexible code which when once formed and adopted can never afterward be improved and enlarged. On the contrary, the intelligent, progressive person will see to it that their table of will values keeps pace with their ever-advancing knowledge and experience.

But here, you should note two very important points of advice and caution concerning proper changes in your table of will values:

1. Never change or modify your scale of will values when under the influence of temptation, or upon the suggestion of others interested in your decision, or when under the fire of opposition.

2. While your scale of will values remains unmodified and unimpaired concerning any decision or choice of a course of action, you should live up to it implicitly and positively. It must be strictly adhered to until modified in the proper manner, and under the proper circumstances—free from outside urge or temptation, suggestion, or opposition.

The following additional advice concerning these points doubtless will be of assistance to you:

Never Change Under Fire

As we have said, your table of will values should never be changed or modified while you are "under fire" either of temptation, direct opposition, or the suggestions of others. All your changes, modifications, and evolutionary developments in your table of will values should be made by you when you are free from the direct influences just referred to. This is because when under the direct influence of these psychological forces your judgment is not always perfectly clear, and your emotional nature often is agitated.

Here is the rule: The changes and modifications—those amendments to your constitution of will—should be made only under the same (or similar) circumstances, and with the same care, consideration, deliberation and subjection to tests, which were involved when you made the decisions leading to the original formation of your table of will values—your constitution of will. By observing this rule you will keep your feet on solid rock and will escape many dangers and unpleasant experiences.

Live by It

Again, we have told you that you should stand by and live up to your existing table of will values at all times. So long as your scale remains unmodified and unimpaired concerning any particular course of action, you should regard it as absolutely binding upon your will and judgment at that time. Any other course would lead you into that state of instability and uncertainty, of indecision and lack of determination, which is the mark of the weak and flabby will.

Your table of will values represents the best that is in you—the best in the whole of your nature—at any given time, and, consequently, in the long run it will be found to be by far the safest and the sanest guide to your actions and decisions. It represents you, yourself, in your state of calm and careful knowledge and decision—as contrasted with you, yourself, under the disturbing influences that shake your judgment and disturb the waters of your emotions. It represents the judgment of "Philip sober" as contrasted with that of "Philip drunk."

Note this distinction, however: Though the stubborn, bigoted person stands by his table of will values, he does not let the law of evolution play upon the same—he admits no new ideas, no new viewpoints, no new facts arising from changed circumstances. The person of true firmness and stability of will, however, while likewise standing firmly by his table of will values, nevertheless always is willing and anxious to "keep up with the times" in his table of values; and he is always working to improve its quality under the proper conditions. While both stand by their table of will values as they exist at the time on all occasions, there is a difference as wide as the distance between the poles in their respective methods. In one case the code is petrified and rigid, while in the other it is flexible, alive, and subject to improvement under the proper conditions. The person who really is "firm" is fixed in purpose, but they are willing to change their position when their purpose is thereby served. The "stubborn" person, however, is fixed only in position—they stick to their position even if their purpose is imperiled and destroyed thereby. Note the distinction.

The above-stated two cautionary rules will be found to work out well in practice, in the long run—the few exceptions, or apparent exceptions, serve principally to emphasize the general rule. There are but very few cases in which these rules will not prove to be the formulae of the wisest and sanest action and conduct. If you have exercised due care in building up your table of will values, the exceptions to these rules will prove to be remarkably small—so small, in fact, that they may be said not to count in the sum total of your experiences.

This system based upon the table of will values is not nearly so arbitrary as it may seem at first glance. Inasmuch as your table of will values has been built carefully, and as carefully passed upon in final decision, it represents the best in your emotional being, your intellectual being, your moral being. This being so, it follows that in living up to these highest reports of your whole being, and in avoiding that which is reported by your whole being as being low and unworthy, you are living up to that which is of the greatest real and permanent value to you—you are being true to yourself, and, according to good authority, in doing this you are also being true to all others.

ESTABLISHING A CONSCIENCE OF WILL VALUES

If you proceed with proper earnestness and determination in the work of building up and establishing your table of will values based upon your chosen fixed standard, and then proceed to apply the standards of that table honestly and conscientiously, then before long you will find that you have established what may be called a *conscience of will values* in your subconscious mental being. This new conscience will grow strong, and will soon manifest itself as strenuously and as efficiently as does the more familiar ordinary "moral conscience" with which all of us are more or less familiar.

The newly awakened conscience of will values in the subconscious regions of your being will sound the alarm-bell when you are in danger of violating the principles of your fixed standard and of failing to observe your top values. It will render you uncomfortable when you are not living up to the requirements of your standards; it will impart the feeling of a warm glow of satisfaction when you comply with the principle. The person in whom this conscience of will values has been awakened is blessed; they will have a "something within" that will keep their feet on the right path and warn them from straying into the bypaths that beset the road of attainment. And thrice blessed is the person who, having this conscience, acquires the habit of steadfastly heeding its warnings and obeying its orders.

This section of this book should be studied in connection with the one immediately preceding it and the one immediately following it, for the three sections are closely related in subject matter, and the instruction in each blends very closely with that in the two others.

In the present section we have considered merely the first phase of the determinative will—the phase of decision or "making up your mind." The consideration of the second phase, the phase of "firm resolve or resolution, or absolute direction to a certain end," will be carried over to the section immediately following the present one—the section dealing with voluntary action. The reason for such division of the subject and such blending of the two phases of will-action will become more apparent to you as we proceed.

CHAPTER 6

ACTIVE WILL

The stage of action is the fifth stage of the will process. Here will manifests in voluntary action—"the process of acting and moving by willpower." This is the final stage of the will process—the stage to which all the preceding stages have been preliminaries. In voluntary action the will manifests its unique character and nature. All the energies of the will have been directed toward voluntary action. Willpower essentially is concerned with action. All human actions are caused by will. Whenever emotion rises to motive and action, that motive and action is will-action. Will is inevitably involved in all *doing*. The motor element of ideas is obtained from will.

Theoretically, it may be said that decision and determination complete the process of will—and, indeed, the old psychologists so held and taught. But practical experience, supported by the teaching of the new psychology, insists that decisions and determinations are of little real value unless they proceed into action. The old saying that "the road to hell is paved with good intentions" might well be altered in its phrasing to read that the pathway to inferno is paved with "non-completed good decisions and aborted resolutions." Many people are in the habit of thinking that when they decide and resolve to do a thing, then the matter is ended, and they need do nothing else in the matter.

It is very easy to sit in a comfortable armchair and resolve that you will do thus-and-so in the world of action; but it is quite difficult to perform even one-tenth of the deeds you may thus resolve and decide to do—though many people do not seem to perceive the distinction and difference between the two processes. As William James has told us, you lie abed on a cold morning and firmly resolve to get up and begin the work of the day; you decide that this is the only rational course to pursue, and you make up your mind to follow it—but often you do not even stir a muscle toward that action. In such cases it is only when the idea of getting up becomes disturbingly insistent—when your mental alarm clock rings most annoyingly and persistently—that you spring out of bed with a final protesting growl and grumble.

The world is filled with people who are unable to realize that deciding and resolving to do a thing is a far different matter from actually doing it. These people seldom accomplish any real work of their own volition—all that they do they are forced to do by others or by the force of circumstances. They are always deciding to do things, resolving to do things—but they never actually do things. Their will-processes are seldom completed. The men and women who do the work of the world, who achieve success, who accomplish their ends and aims, are those who, having grimly resolved and determined to do a certain thing, then complete the will-process by moving into action in the direction of doing the thing in question.

But here, again, we meet with another of those strange paradoxes with which the science of psychology abounds. We have just seen that if you expect to accomplish anything in the world you must pass beyond the stage of mere decision, resolution, and determination—you must rise to the plane of voluntary action. But, on the other hand, if you expect your voluntary action to "amount to anything," to be efficient, to accomplish its purpose, you must carry into your voluntary action a highly developed form of determination. In fact, when closely analyzed, voluntary action is purposeful determination manifesting its dynamic aspect. The subjective phase of determination is the static aspect of will; objective voluntary action is the dynamic aspect of will; the two are twin aspects of the same thing.

Once you understand this fact, it follows that your effective voluntary action must always be preceded and accompanied by strong, positive, purposeful determination. Let me here repeat the definition of this term. The term *purpose* means: "The view, aim, design, intention, determination, resolution, or will to accomplish or reach some particular object; that which a person sets before themselves as the object to be gained or accomplished; the end or aim which one has in view in any plan, measure, or exertion; that which one intends to do, hence, their intention, design, plan or project." The term *determination*, in this particular usage, is defined as: "Strength or firmness of mind; firm resolve or resolution; an absolute direction to a certain end."

From the above definitions you will have no difficulty in forming a dear and positive concept of purposeful determination; but for the purpose of illustration I ask you to consider, ponder over, and memorize the following quotations from eminent writers. Each of these has been selected for a special purpose and to awaken and bring out a certain phase of your willpower. They will help you to fill in the details of your mental picture or general idea of purposeful determination, that essential spirit of will.

> Buxton says: "The longer I live, the more certain I am that the great difference between men, between the feeble and the powerful, the great and the insignificant, is invincible determination—a purpose once fixed, and then victory or death. That quality will do anything that can be done in this world—and no talents, no circumstances, no opportunities, will make a two-legged creature a man without it."

Mitchell says: "Resolve is what makes a man manifest; not a puny resolve, not errant purpose—but that strong and indefatigable will which treads down difficulties and danger as a boy treads down the heaving frost lands of winter; which kindles his eye and brain with a pulse-beat toward the unattainable. will makes men giants."

Disraeli says: "I have brought myself by long meditation to the conviction that a human being with a settled purpose must accomplish it, and that nothing can resist a will which will stake even existence itself upon its fulfillment."

Simpson says: "A passionate desire, and an unwearied will, can perform impossibilities, or what may seem to be such to the cold and feeble."

Foster says: "It is wonderful to note how even the casualties of life seem to bow to a spirit that will not yield to them, and tend to subserve a design which they may, in their apparent tendency, threaten to frustrate. When a firm, decisive spirit is recognized, it is curious to see how the space clears around a man and leaves him room and freedom."

Emerson says: "We go forth austere, dedicated, believing in iron links of destiny, and will not turn on our heels to save our lives. A book, a bust, or only the sound of a name shoots a spark through the nerves, and we suddenly believe in will. We cannot hear of personal vigor of any kind, great powers of performances, without fresh resolution."

This, then, is the spirit in which you should institute your voluntary actions leading to the achievement and realization of your prime motives, your top values, your fixed standard, your *summum bonum* or chief good. You should approach your task in the spirit of the master formula of attainment:

1. Definite Ideals

2. Insistent Desire

3. Confident Expectation

4. Persistent Determination

5. Balanced Compensation

Consider carefully the principles of this master formula, which you are about to employ in your task of voluntary action leading toward achievement. Consider in detail its elements, as these are presented to you in the following several pages; ponder them carefully; commit to memory their essential points.

1. DEFINITE IDEALS

Before you may proceed intelligently to do a thing, to obtain a thing, or to achieve a thing, it is necessary that you have a clear and definite idea of that thing. In your consideration of purposeful determination, you must not lose sight of the importance of *purpose* while you are developing *determination*. Determination will lose much of its dynamic force if it is scattered, or if the purpose directing it lacks definiteness and clearness. Remember that one of the definitions of *determination* is, "Absolute direction to a certain end" and that *purpose* means: "The aim, design, intention, resolution, determination and will to accomplish or to reach some particular object or end."

Note particularly the reference to "a certain end" and to "some particular object or end." The words *certain* and *particular* imply definiteness, clearness, preciseness, specificness of meaning, and ideals. They point to the necessity of definite ideals and definite purpose. If definite direction is lacking in your voluntary action, then your purposeful determination has lost one of its strong arms. This first element of the master formula is very important in the case before us—the case of manifesting voluntary action and purposeful determination.

Before you can really determine to act effectively, you must know the purpose of your action—the end to be attained, the thing to be obtained, or the direction in which you wish to travel. The more definite and positive your purpose and aim, the greater will be the degree of concentration that you are able to apply to the task. Here you must bring to bear your powers of visualization. You must learn to map out the land over which you are to travel—to chart the seas over which you wish to sail. You must exercise your constructive ability in designing, planning, mapping out, and making a working diagram of what you wish to accomplish. You know the general direction by reason of your knowledge of your prime motives, top values, and fixed standard; but probably you have not drawn your plan in further detail and filled in all of the minor points. You must correct and overcome this deficiency, if it exists in your case.

You may find it impossible to draw your plans in very close detail, however. In such case, do the best you can; draw the general outline as clearly as possible, and then fill in the details from time to time as soon as they take form in your constructive imagination. Do the best you can in the creation of a definite purpose—a little practice will enlarge your capacity for work of this kind. You would not expect a builder to erect a house for you unless he were supplied with a working plan by the architect; you would not expect a railroad contractor to build a line or road for you unless he were furnished with the plans of the engineer for such construction. Therefore, you must know positively, clearly, and definitely what you wish to accomplish—the ends and aims to be attained, the direction of your efforts, the

particular purpose you wish to work out into achievement—before you can expect to apply effectively your
persistent determination.

It is not scientific for you to sing, "I don't know where
I'm going, but I'm on the way." You must know where
you're going—not only that, you must also know for just
what purpose you are going there and what you are likely
to meet with on the road. You must take a lesson from the
old story of the architect on the witness stand: He stated
that a person of his profession was required to plan every
building. The opposing lawyer sneeringly asked him: "Pray
tell us, then, who was the architect of the Tower of Babel?"
The architect promptly answered: "There was none, sir;
hence the confusion and failure."

By reference to the earlier quotations, you will see that
the quoted writers have laid special emphasis upon "the
purpose well fixed," "the settled purpose," and "the design."
Disraeli's statement that "a human being with a settled
purpose must accomplish it" gives us the keynote. The purpose must not only be clear and definite, but it also must
be a fixed and settled purpose—a purpose adhered to with
dogged persistency and determined steadfastness. The
more clearly you can see just what you want to do, the better you will be able to do it, and the more determined you
will be to materialize that idealized and visualized purpose.

You must not only "want to hard enough," but you
must also "know just what you want"—to know it clearly

enough and definitely enough. Possessing and manifesting these powers of your mental and emotional being, you are prepared to apply and to exercise your purposeful determination to its utmost capacity and with its full powers. Having discovered your purpose in life, you must proceed to manifest it in voluntary action and to materialize it—the more definite and clear the mental picture, the more definite and positive will be the materialization.

2. INSISTENT DESIRE

You have become acquainted with the facts concerning the power of desire. You have seen that all willpower is set into operation by desire, and that the degree of manifested willpower is directly proportionate to the degree of the desire behind it. This being so, you need no further argument concerning the necessity of manifesting strong, positive desire when you wish to accomplish anything. You realize that the flame of desire is needed to generate the steam of voluntary action.

In order to attain your top values, prime motives, or the manifestation of your fixed standard, you should ever seek to manifest that insistent, imperious, dominant feeling and desire that will not be denied. I have repeatedly illustrated this mental state with the example of the drowning or suffocating person demanding air; the starving person demanding food; the shipwrecked or desert-lost person demanding water; the wild creature demanding its mate; the mother creature demanding the safety and welfare of its young. This is the spirit of insistent desire in which you should approach your task of voluntary action toward the attainment of your prime motives and top values.

3. CONFIDENT EXPECTATION

The mental state represented by the term *confident expectation* is one of positive value to you. Its opposite, the mental state of fearful doubt, is most harmful to you. Confident expectation tends to release into activity all the powers of your mental being and to fill them with that eagerness for accomplishment which is based upon confidence and belief in the final successful outcome. Fear and doubt tend to paralyze the will, while faith and hope tend to energize and inspire it. We need not go into the psychology of this fact here—the statement of the fact itself is sufficient, and the reference to common experience illustrates its operations.

If you will consider the cases of the men and women who have accomplished great things in the world, along any of the many lines of human endeavor, you will see that in every case such individuals have been inspired by the belief in their ultimate success—they have confidently expected a successful outcome. Had they believed otherwise, they would not have had the courage and perseverance that enabled them to overcome the obstacles in their path and to mount to success upon the stepping-stones of their own apparent failures.

It is confident expectation—that combination of faith and hope—which enables one to act upon the adage, "When you feel that you must let go—then hang on the harder, for victory is near." When we realize the effect of confident expectation upon the will-activities, we are almost impelled to agree fully with the celebrated statement, "To believe firmly is almost tantamount to accomplishment." But whether or not this principle may be carried that far, it is unquestionable that confident expectation is a most powerful and mighty element in successful and effective voluntary action.

In this instruction we have urged the adoption of the slogan: "I can, I will; I dare, I do!" The "I can" is based upon confident expectation; the "I dare" springs from the same inner conviction of ultimate success. In fact, the spirit of confident expectation breathes through and pervades the whole of the slogan—and all the processes of the awakened will.

4. PERSISTENT DETERMINATION

Here we approach the characteristic element of purposeful determination. The very word *determination* carries with it the idea of "persistency." The idea of persistency is present in all applications of the "I can, I will; I dare, I do!" maxim. There must always be present not only the determination to do the thing, but also the persistent application of the will to the task. Determination without persistency would be like the play of Hamlet with the character of Hamlet omitted. In fact, it is difficult to form a concept of practical willpower unless we include in the concept the element of active persistency. The persistent will is the effective will— the real will in action. Whatever else we may conceive effective will to be, we must always conceive it as being persistent.

In persistent determination you manifest willpower not only in voluntary action, but also in the task of steadying and holding the dynamic power of will to its work. When you have gained complete control of your aroused willpower, you must apply to its activities the quality of persistence. This quality you must manifest in steadfastness, firmness, fixed intention, positive direction, and unfailing constancy in continuing the course chosen. You must manifest it by steadfastly pursuing the work undertaken and holding fast to the general plan designed to govern that work. You must manifest it in perseverance, in spite of obstacles and discouragements, and in steadfastness in the face of opposition and hindrances.

The characteristics of persistent determination are stability, perseverance, fixedness of purpose, tenacity, doggedness, and persistent application. Persistent determination enables you to hold your will close to its task—to hold it there firmly and continuously until success is attained and the victory is won. Success in many instances depends upon the application of persistent determination—the manifestation of the power and determination to hold on to the last. Many a person possessing the other qualities of willpower has fought a brave fight, but just before the tide turned in their favor they relinquished their efforts and dropped out of the fight—defeated, not by circumstances, but by their own lack of persistent determination. By studying the lives of the great inventors—Morse and Edison, for instance—you will see the utmost importance of this faculty of "holding on" and this spirit of "never say die."

5. BALANCED COMPENSATION

This element of the master formula finds its familiar expression in the phrase *paying the price*. In all attainment, the price must be paid. Compensation is a law of nature and manifests its force on all planes of existence, in all forms of activity. One who seeks to attain anything must be prepared to pay the price. The price may consist of work performed—perseverance, persistent application, industry, and diligence—or service rendered to others with whom one has business or similar relations. It may consist of ability and willingness to give value received for what you obtain for yourself; of the sacrifice and renunciation of ideas, ideals, feelings, desires, aims and ambitions that are opposed to the prime motives and top values. You must be willing to sacrifice the lesser values for the greater ones.

All who achieve anything worthwhile have paid the price in all of the various forms just mentioned. Compensation is necessary for attainment; there is always a

balance struck between what a person gets and what they give or give up. Anyone who seeks to escape paying the price is defying a great law of nature and of life. It is as if in the cosmos there were maintained a great ledger, in which there is both a credit and a debit column on each page. The law is continually striking balances, trial balances, and final settlements. The wise realize this and profit by their knowledge; the fools ignore it and are the losers by reason of their folly. "Say the gods to men: 'What do you want? Take it, and pay for it!'"

THE SPIRIT OF THE ACTIVE WILL

The following quotations from eminent writers will serve to illustrate the spirit of the active will, particularly in its phase of purposeful determination. You should consider each of the quotations carefully, ponder them earnestly, and commit them to memory. Each one of them has been selected for the purpose of bringing out some particular point or principle, and each and all of them are designed to serve as an inspirational maxim for you in moments of trial, temptation, doubt, or discouragement—they are veritable potions of will tonic. I defy you to repeat them earnestly without feeling the vibrations and thrill of will stirring your soul and awakening the spirit of "I can, I will; I dare, I do!"

Kennan says: "In this world, the human spirit with its dominating force, the will, may be and ought to be superior to all bodily sensations and all accidents of environment."

Harriet Beecher Stowe says: "When you get into a tight place and everything goes against you until it seems that you cannot hold on for a minute longer, never give up then, for that is just the place and time that the tide will turn."

D'Alembert says: "Go on, sir, go on! The difficulties you meet with will resolve themselves as you advance. Proceed, and the light will dawn, and shine with increasing clearness on your path."

Henry Ward Beecher says: "It is defeat that turns bone to flint, and gristle to muscle and makes men invincible, and formed those heroic natures that are now in ascendency in the world. Do not be afraid of defeat. You are never so near victory as when defeated in a good cause."

Cuyler says: "It is astonishing how many men lack the power of 'holding on' until they reach the goal. They can make a sudden dash, but they lack grit. They are easily discouraged. They get on as long as everything moves smoothly, but when there is friction they lose heart. They depend upon stronger personalities for their spirit and strength. They lack independence or originality. They only dare to do what others do. They do not step boldly from the crowd and act fearlessly."

Emerson says: "I know no such unquestionable badge and ensign of a sovereign mind as that of tenacity of purpose, which, through all changes of companions or parties or fortunes, changes never, bates no jot of heart or hope, but wearies out opposition and arrives at its port."

John Hunter says: "Is there one whom difficulties dishearten, who bends to the storm? He will do little. Is there one who wills to conquer? That kind of man never fails."

Napoleon Bonaparte said: "The truest wisdom is a resolute determination."

Munger says: "A strong defiant purpose is many-handed, and lays hold on whatever is near that can serve it; it has a magnetic power that draws to itself whatever is kindred."

Wirt says: "The man who is perpetually hesitating which of two things he will do first will do neither. The man who resolves, but suffers his resolution to be changed by the first counter-suggestion of a friend—who fluctuates from opinion to opinion, from plan to plan, and veers like a weathercock to every point of the compass, with every breath of caprice that blows—can never accomplish any-thing real or useful. It is only the man who first consults well, then resolves firmly, and then executes his purposes with inflexible perseverance, undismayed by those petty difficulties which daunt a weaker spirit—that man can advance to eminence in any line."

Fothergill says: "Willpower is one of the greatest nat-ural endowments—as it is one of the finest outcomes of self-culture. The man who succeeds in climbing, step by step, finds his willpower expanding with his energies, with the demands upon him. Strength of will is gameness—the power to 'stay.' Englishmen have always prided themselves upon their game qualities; whether the tenacity of their bulldogs, the endurance of their race horses, the unflinch-ing courage of their game-fowls, or their own indomitable purpose. 'Where there's a will, there's a way.' The way may be long hidden from sight, hard to find, long and weari-some, seemingly endless; but on it the traveler goes with unshaken resolution—to success at last."

In purposeful determination and voluntary action, the will deliberately chooses an end or object to be attained and then proceeds to manifest the determination in out-ward form and action. It proceeds to its end with intensity of purpose and directness of aim. The end must be clear, definite, and capable of distinct visualization. The effort to gain that end must call into operation the whole nature of the will and the whole force and energy of the willpower.

As it has well been said: "The whole, living strength of the will must be literally hurled into it, not once or twice, but again and again, until it is accomplished."

The purposeful determination must be real—it must be meant by you with the full power of your soul. You must not trifle with such resolutions; you must be in deadly earnest about them. Remember that the honor and integrity of your will is at stake, and that you must not bring discredit upon it. To break such a resolution is to bring shame upon yourself and to your will. You will do well to remember and to follow the advice given by a religious writer upon the subject who bids his pupils to proceed to will by first making the following statement:

"Yes! Before God, I mean that! I mean it as intensely and really as I can ever mean anything! I will keep that resolution. I know that I can and will keep it, because I mean it. Further, I will take every precaution to keep it alive and vigorous within me by remaking it again and again."

This is the essence and spirit of purposeful determination. Strive ever to attain, sustain, and manifest it. *This is the flash of the will that can!*

CHAPTER 7

WILL TRAINING

It is not enough that you develop strong willpower, important as such a development is. It is not enough that the driver secure the services of a strong pair of horses to pull his chariot—he must also be able to guide and control, direct and master them. So, though you may be possessed of the strongest will, you will be unable to direct efficiently its energies and powers unless you have mastered its mechanism by careful, scientific training and discipline. To "train" your will, you must teach it and cultivate it; you must educate it, exercise it, discipline it so as to impart to it the habit and tendency to move along the lines your reason indicates to be the most advantageous and efficient.

All scientific training of the will begins with forming advantageous habits—building clean and clear paths over which the will may travel in action toward achievement. By establishing the proper habits of will-action, you will render your will far more efficient, and at the same time will accomplish maximum desirable results with minimal energy expenditure. Here we meet with another of those interesting paradoxes which, as we have said, abound in the realm of psychology. The paradox is: 1) the will moves most easily and with the least friction over the paths of habit, yet 2) habit itself is originally formed by the exercise of the will.

The will lends itself most readily to habit and prefers to travel over the lines of least resistance in habit-motivity; yet, when set to the task, the will builds the lines and paths of advantageous and desirable habits over which it will travel in the future. It acts like the strong and powerful stream of water, which first cuts for itself a deep channel in the earth, and afterward travels through that channel as if bound and restricted by it. Both the stream and the will are bound and restricted by their self-built channels—but each creates for itself its future restricting and directing walls.

Habit has its correspondence in material objects; in fact, all things seem to come under the rule of habit in some form. A piece of paper, or a pattern of cloth, will tend to fold more easily along the lines of the crease made by the first folding. The more often the fold is made, the easier becomes each subsequent fold. Water finds it easier to travel over the path traversed by the preceding streams of water; the raindrop on the window pane follows the same law.

Any voluntary action performed several times in the same general way tends to develop into a motion-habit; and, indeed, after a time the motion becomes almost instinctive and is performed by the subconscious, to which it has been passed on for attention and direction. Each and every time you dress yourself or put on your shoes, you perform a number of habitual actions of which you are scarcely conscious. This is also true of your actions of walking, using your knife and fork, and other familiar performances that have become habitual to you.

The value of habit in the training and education of the will is very great. Not only does habit *simplify* the process of any given action and *lessen* the degree of voluntary attention required, but it also *gives greatly increased weight and power* to the emotional impulse toward any given action. Thus habit increases the emotional value of action and enables it to resist more effectively any opposing emotional impulses and desires. When you have made a habit of efficient and advantageous will-action, you will have progressed far on the road to the attainment of strong and efficient willpower.

RULES FOR ESTABLISHING HABITS OF WILL

The following rules will be most useful and effective in your task of establishing the proper habits of will. In applying them you must employ your table of will values and your fixed standard to determine which particular habits you shall strive to develop, cultivate, and acquire. When in the following rules you come across the words *the habit* or *habits*, you will understand that such terms apply to habits that express the desires (tested by reason) that stand well at the top of your table of will values—or else to minor courses of will-action that serve to further the interests of these high values. Here are the rules:

1. Employ a Strong Initiative

In launching a new habit, employ a strong initiative. Put as much determination and motor energy as possible into the particular course of action, at the start. Launch the ship of habit as far as possible into the stream of action, employing the full strength of the determination and will-force at your command. This will impart to the new habit sufficient momentum to carry it well past the first dangerous places and to give you a good "running start." Your principal danger of yielding to temptation will come at the start; but if your momentum is sufficient to carry you past these earlier temptations, you will be able more easily to resist the later ones. The longer you manage to postpone the time of the first temptations, the less power will those temptations have over you. Therefore, always remember, try to get a good running start.

2. Exercise Care at the Beginning

Beginning to form a new habit is the most critical time of the entire task. This because the power of the opposing habit has not begun to fade yet. The rule is: Never allow even a single exception or failure to occur until the new habit has become well-established. Until the new habit has become well rooted, you must brave it with all your power against the stormy winds of temptation and opposition. It has well been said that failure or yielding to temptation at this early stage is like dropping the ball of string you have been carefully winding—the single slip undoes more than many turns of the hand will be able to re-wind.

The psychology of the case is this: The two opposing impulses must be handled so that the advantageous one may have an uninterrupted series of successes, and the disadvantageous one a continuous series of failures. These preliminary conflicts play a very important part in determining the future of the two opposing forces. Here the rule applies: "to him who hath shall be given, and to him who hath not shall be taken away even that which he hath." Once the habit of victory is acquired, it will thereafter possess an immense psychological advantage over its repeatedly defeated opponent.

The person who determines to establish a certain advantageous habit will surely fail if they follow Rip Van Winkle's plan of saying that "this one doesn't count" whenever tempted to violate the rule. Taking "just one" cigar when you have decided to stop smoking, or taking "just one" little extra snooze when you have decided to establish the habit of rising at a certain hour, may undo the entire purposeful determination. On the other hand, each time you resist one of those "just one more" indulgences, your purposeful determination becomes stronger—often far more than the actual value of the accomplishment.

3. Repeated Performance

In establishing a habit, you should repeat the performance of the associated action as frequently as possible. You will by that means make clearer and wider the mental path over which you wish your will to travel habitually. Moreover, as a consequence, you will exercise the particular faculty you wish to strengthen and develop. The will is strengthened not by the mere mental determination to perform an action, but rather by the actual performance of the action itself. The path of motive is created only by actually travelling over it. The oftener it is travelled, the easier becomes the future journey. The actual motor-effect of will-action *sets* the brain cells and areas involved into the particular course of action.

The actual effort forces you to dig your heels in the ground and to exert your energy. As it has well been said: "He who has no solid ground to press against will never get beyond the stage of gesture-making." Therefore, seek every possible opportunity for such action until the habit becomes firmly established. A lock works better after it has been used several times; a shoe fits better after it has been worn a few times; the paper folds more easily in the crease after it has been folded a few times; and as an old writer once said: "Continued action is like a stream of water, which wears for itself a channel from which it may not easily be turned."

4. Control the Attention

So far as possible, do not allow your attention to dwell upon actions opposed to your new habit; keep your attention fixed, so far as is possible, upon ideas associated with your new habit. Thus you will feed one set of motor-ideas and starve the opposite set. If you are trying to break yourself of the habit of smoking, you are very foolish if you allow your mind to dwell upon the pleasures of the pipe, cigar, or cigarette; instead, hold mental pictures of the advantages of refraining from smoking. Above all, hold firmly before your mind the idea that you are demonstrating that you have a will strong enough to enable you to break an undesirable habit.

You will do well (particularly at first) to follow the example of the companions of Ulysses, who stopped their ears with wax that they might not hear the seductive voices of the sirens. The voyagers who neglected this precaution were lured to their destruction, because they allowed the tempting sounds to enter their ears. This is not cowardice, but the part of courage, when rightly understood. "He jests at scars, who never felt a wound." As has well been said: "It takes more courage to turn away from some ideas than to face them, and the coward is sometimes he who remains on the scene."

One of the most effective methods of neutralizing the power of a threatening desire or impulse is deliberately changing the direction of your attention. It is an axiom of psychology that: "While attention follows interest, nevertheless, attention may be directed by a determined act of will so as to arouse interest not previously present; this interest, so awakened, rises to desire, and desire gives motive-power and direction to will." In this axiom we have the key to the problem we are now considering.

It is a well-established fact of psychology that, in the processes of the deliberative and determinative will, whatever attracts and holds the attention will have greater weight and power than would otherwise be the case. The interesting alternative holds the more favorable position, while the uninteresting one is pushed to the side—sometimes unjustly. This process is akin to what we experience in ourselves when we prefer a political candidate we know and like, rather than one unfamiliar to us who does not arouse our interested attention.

In view of this fact, you can see how important it is to direct and hold your attention upon the course of action that your reason and your table of will values shows to be the best one; and to shut out of your attention the opposing alternative. By doing this, you give to the advantageous idea the added strength of attention and interest, and you place the objectionable idea in the far less favorable position.

Many people have prevented themselves from acting foolishly and wrongfully by determinedly turning their attention to the consequences of the harmful action. It has been called a master stroke of the battle of inhibition to consider the benefits of a contrary action or mentally picture the evil effects of the desired action. The drunkard thinking of his sick child at home is strengthened in his effort to inhibit the urge of his appetite. The more Macbeth and his wife held in mind and pictured in imagination the idea of fame and power, the stronger grew their desire and determination to kill the king. Their attention developed increased interest and desire, and thus heightened the power of the original motive.

The will is able to determine which of the motives influencing it shall become the stronger; it accomplishes this by deciding which of two ideas shall occupy the field of attention during the desire-conflict. Emotion and desire develop under the stimulus of attention. As the master of attention, the will has the power to encourage or to banish the ideas calling forth the emotional feeling and the resulting desires. If you keep one set of ideas in your field of attention, a strong emotional interest and desire may gather around it; but if you call the opposite set of ideas into your field of attention and hold it firmly there, then the first set of ideas will lose your interest and motive power.

This principle is illustrated in one of Moliere's comedies. Jeppe, a dissolute character, is sent by his wife (a washer-woman) to the village shop to buy a piece of soap, and is entrusted with a small coin for that purpose. But Jeppe wants a drink. He knows that his wife will beat him if he wastes the money, but he also knows that he has a strong craving for the glass of wine. A desire-conflict ensues. Jeppe says to himself: "My stomach says wine, my back says soap." He is torn by the internal struggle.

Finally, as he walks along, he sees the tavern ahead of him. This decides the conflict—the object in the field of attention proves stronger than that which is outside the field. He says: "Is not a man's stomach more to him than his back? Yes, say I!" and into the tavern he walks. Had he but looked around the corner and seen his wife wearing a look of determination on her face and carrying a big stick in her hand as she marched after him, he would have decided in favor of his back rather than his stomach. The two sets of desires and impulses were nicely balanced in the case of Jeppe, but the added element of aroused attention and interest brought the victory for the wine and the defeat of the soap.

RULES FOR WILL TRAINING

The following rules for the direction of attention will be useful in will training, particularly in inhibiting and restraining the unwelcome desires and impulses that pull against the high values and the fixed standard:

1. Feed the Positives

Feed the will with ideas and mental pictures favorably representing the desires and actions that constitute the top values of your table of will values, which are in accord with your fixed standard.

2. Starve the Negatives

Starve the disadvantageous desires and impulses and their resulting actions by resolutely refusing to allow your attention to be directed toward ideas and mental pictures that favor the bottom values of your table of will values, which are in opposition to your fixed standard.

3. The Law of Opposites

In cultivating an advantageous desire or impulse and its resulting action, resolutely refuse to allow your attention and imagination to become occupied with ideas and mental pictures favoring the opposite desires, impulses, and actions. In restraining, inhibiting, or neutralizing a dis-advantageous desire, deliberately and determinedly direct your attention and imagination upon the ideas and mental pictures that favor the opposing (advantageous) set of desires and impulses and their resulting actions.

The reason for the above is: 1) attention and interest feed desires and impulses and strengthen ideas; lack of attention and interest starve them; 2) by bestowing attention and interest upon one set of desires, you tend to inhibit, weaken, and starve the opposite set. Both of these facts are highly important.

EXERCISES IN WILL TRAINING

Observing the rules stated above will give your will valuable exercise in will training. In addition to these, however, there are several general exercises that will prove of great value to you in strengthening the fiber of your will and developing your powers of steadfastness, resolution, and determination. By exercising your will against obstacles, opposition, and hindrances—those existing in the outer world, and those that have their abode in your inner world of habit, desire, and impulse—you give to your will a resisting power and an aggressive force in the conduct of your everyday life when you are required to assert your willpower and strength of will. The following principles and methods of will training are directed to these ends.

TEMPERING THE WILL ALONG THE LINES OF RESISTANCE

Practical thinkers have known for centuries that one of the best possible exercises to develop strong willpower is deliberate and determined performance of certain selected unpleasant tasks. These tasks are carried out not necessarily because of any actual immediate value to oneself or others, but rather solely and simply as valuable exercise and training of the will.

Many ancient teachers began the instruction of their pupils in this way. The result of the persistent practice of this method, under the intelligent guidance of the teachers, developed and trained the pupils into veritable giants of willpower. The world-renowned Jesuit order has for hundreds of years employed similar methods for the purpose of strengthening the wills of their students; as a result, the Jesuits are renowned for their powers of determination, persistency, and endurance.

Many of the best modern psychologists have revived this old teaching and its methods, and references to the principle may be found in many of the textbooks of the modern masters of this branch of science. For instance, the following statement of William James, one of the best practical philosophers and psychologists of modern times:

> Keep the faculty alive by a little gratuitous exercise every day. That is, be systematically ascetic or heroic in little unnecessary points; do every day something for no other reason than that you would rather not do it, so that when the hour of dire need draws nigh, it may find you not unnerved and untrained to stand the test.

> The man who has daily inured himself to habits of concentrated attention, energetic volition, and self-denial in unnecessary things will stand like a tower when everything rocks around him, and when his softer fellow mortals are winnowed like chaff in the blast.Says Eliphas Levi:

> By means of persevering and gradual athletics the powers of the body may be developed to an amazing extent. It is the same with the powers of the soul. Would you govern yourself and others? Learn how to will! How may one learn to will? Strength cannot prove itself except by conquest. Idleness and negligence are the enemies of will; and this is the reason why all religions have multiplied their practices and made their cults difficult and minute. The more trouble one

gives himself for an idea, the more power one acquires in regard to that idea. Hence the power of religions resides entirely in the inflexible will of those who practice them.Accustoming the will to face disagreeable tasks and overcome disagreeable conditions by sheer determination is one of the very best systems of schooling and tempering the will. By accustoming the will to act in this way, you will school it so that it will act efficiently when similar conditions arise in actual life. This has well been called "tempering the will along the lines of the greatest resistance." The will trained in this way is always ready to meet disagreeable emergencies, no matter how suddenly they may present themselves, nor how serious they may be.

It has well been said of people trained in this way that while others are crying over spilt milk, the possessors of trained wills are hunting for another cow to milk, or may even have found such a cow and have actually begun to milk her. On the other hand, the person who carefully and habitually endeavors to escape unpleasant tasks, disagreeable facts, and uncomfortable circumstances lacks such preparatory training of their will. When they are actually confronted with disagreeable circumstances or disastrous conditions, their will isn't equal to the task of overcoming them. Those who have pushed and elbowed their way to the front ranks of endeavor in any walk of life have developed wills of this kind. Some of them have obtained the development by strenuous experiences in "the university of hard knocks," while others have anticipated and forestalled this by scientific preparation before the day of the actual examination.

Life is filled with disagreeable tasks and uncomfortable circumstances; to perform the first and to master the second requires the trained will. Wise is the one who learns their lesson before the hour of trial—they are doubly armed for the fray. Training of this kind has been likened to fire insurance on a house—it costs something in effort and self-denial, but it is something laid by for the hour of need. It is the great reserve fund of habitual will-action upon which you can draw in the time of necessity. The importance of such training cannot be overestimated. It is like starting and maintaining an account in a good savings bank—you add to it little by little, and you accumulate rapidly by reason of the compound interest drawn by your deposits.

A well-known teacher advised his pupils to do something occasionally for no other reason than that they "would rather not do it," if it were no more than giving up a seat in a street car. Napoleon had a will trained along these lines; his will was so completely under his control that apparently without any emotional struggle he could enter upon courses of disagreeable, difficult, and unpleasant action, even though they involved the greatest hardships.

You will find numerous opportunities to exercise your will along this line of training—every day will furnish you with such. Do something that you particularly dislike to do—do it not because there is any special merit in the doing, but solely and simply because of the training it will give your will. A certain man was discovered one day carefully studying John Stuart Mill's great work *Principles of Political Economy*—a subject he loathed and for which he lost no opportunity to express his aversion. When asked why he was doing this, he replied: "I am training my will; I am doing this because I dislike it intensely."

The great men and women of history have trained their wills along lines of the greatest resistance, while the average men and women have been content to exercise their will only along the lines of the least resistance. The former have so trained themselves that when they are required to perform some disagreeable action, they do so with as much ease and force as if the action were most agreeable to them. The latter find it almost impossible to perform disagreeable actions except by whipping and spurring themselves to the task, and even then they perform the action only half-heartedly and with little force or effectiveness. I advise you to master this feature of your will training. The day will come when you will thank me from the bottom of your heart for this advice, provided you have followed it.

TEMPERING THE WILL BY SELF-DENIAL

Akin to the preceding exercise is the occasional practice of self-denial—the deliberate denial to yourself of your favorite pleasure. This denial is not to be made because of any direct merit in the sacrifice, but merely because of the exercise of the will and the additional strength acquired by its performance. Many of the penances and other acts of self-denial of the great religions of the world tend to develop willpower in the individual practicing them. This fact is acknowledged by the best authorities, but it is not generally realized by the masses of people practicing the acts in question. The great religious teachers know that the person who has trained their will along the lines of occasional self-denial will find it easier to resist real temptation when it comes to them. Psychology recognizes the practical value in self-denial and penance, aside from their purely religious elements.

The general principles that govern tempering the will by the performance of disagreeable and unpleasant tasks apply also to tempering the will by self-denial. The performance of disagreeable tasks and the act of refraining from something agreeable are alike displeasing to the untrained will. Therefore, the same principle is involved in both, and the will is thereby trained along the same general lines, though the approach is from opposite directions.

In the method of training the will by self-denial, you must deliberately select some pleasant action—something you wish very much to do—and then resolutely refuse to do it within a certain time limit. The denial may involve refusing to smoke your customary after-dinner cigar, to drink your favorite cup of coffee, to read the conclusion of an interesting book or of the new installment of a serial story, to eat some particularly desired and favored dish, to attend some play which you have been very anxious to witness—in fact, the refusal to do any particular thing you earnestly long to do.

The time limit must be definitely fixed and strictly observed. There is a positive psychological value to the definite time limit. You must be absolutely honest in selecting the object of your self-denial—it must involve a real test and must require a real effort of the will to accomplish. You must give up something of real emotional value to yourself—of course, only within the time limits deliberately set at the start. The time limit must be sufficiently extended to afford a real test of the will. The self-denial must "hurt." You must be a severe taskmaster to yourself in these trials, tests, and exercises. There must be no trifling or fooling in the matter. You must set yourself a real job—and you must be the real person to accomplish it.

Note: In each of the two exercises, you will be wise not to select tasks of such a nature that they bring you a comfortable feeling of religious or ethical merit or of "duty well performed." Do not choose anything you are in duty bound to do or not to do, in accordance with your accepted codes of religious, ethical, or moral standards or obligations. Otherwise, you have the positive value of duty or religious or moral obligation to add weight to your resolute determination and its manifestation. In these exercises you should endeavor to select tasks in which the only motive is "the will to will"—to pit the will against the pull of feelings, impulses, and desires. You should deny to yourself the aid of the added weight of duty or obligations. The only reason for the performance of these exercises is to arouse "the will to will"—willing for the sake of willing, merely to prove that it is will.

REVERSING HABITS

A third method, involving the same general principles, is that either 1) of doing something it is your regular habit and custom not to do; or 2) of not doing something which it is your regular habit and custom to do.

In either phase of this exercise, you should select a habit you have no special like or dislike for—something neither especially agreeable or disagreeable, but which you usually do or not do solely because of an established habit. Some little regular habit of dressing, of proceeding to your business by a certain route, of lunching at a certain place or in a certain part of the room, or something of that kind—such are the tasks to be selected. This may seem like silly trifling when you first think of it—but wait until you actually try it! You have a surprise awaiting you. Set a time limit here, as in the other cases.

As a few examples, I suggest the following: After ascertaining which particular shoe (or stocking) you put on first in dressing, deliberately reverse the order for the period of one week. Or, follow the same procedure in the matter of placing your right or your left arm (as the case may be) first in your coat when you put it on—change the order of the arm-placing for the period of one week. Or, again, change the choice of your morning or afternoon newspaper for one day, occasionally. Or, pursue a different route in traveling from one place to another—this is effective only when you have already established the habit of making the daily trip along a certain regular route. If you will exercise your ingenuity, you will discover many little tasks of this kind. In so doing, you will not only train your will along particularly trying lines, but will also learn a valuable lesson concerning the power of habit in everyday life.

PERFORMING UNINTERESTING TASKS

Another method, and one greatly favored in some quarters, is that of deliberately performing some monotonous, purposeless, and uninteresting task—just for the sake of "willing to will." For instance:

1. Sitting on a chair for five minutes, with the arms crossed, and the feet pressed together at the sides of the shoe-soles.

2. Walking to and fro in your room for five minutes, touching a number of articles in regular order as you pass them.

3. Counting and re-counting a number of small articles for five minutes.

4. Changing your chair at every count of twenty-five for five minutes.

5. Reading backward and forward a certain paragraph of a book (this one for instance) for five minutes.

6. Replacing in a box, very slowly and deliberately, one hundred matches, or small pieces of paper.

7. Putting on and taking off a pair of gloves, slowly and deliberately, for five minutes.

The above examples will give you a general idea of the character of this class of exercises, but actual practice of them will be required to show you the amount of persistent resolution and determination required to perform them properly.

TEMPERING THE WILL
BY ASSERTING IT

Another valuable form of will training, but one which must be employed judiciously, is that in which the will is tempered by actual assertion of its power. By assertion I do not mean "to affirm, to aver, to state positively," which is one usage of the term; instead, I mean "to maintain or defend by words or measures, to vindicate." In tempering the will by assertion, you proceed to assert your will in little things, so as to have your own way about such things irrespective of actual benefit. The sole object is to habituate the will to having its way, and thereby to give it confidence in itself and to build up the habit of success. You will find that you have been in the habit of giving way to others in the little things solely because it has been too much trouble to make an effort of will in the opposite direction. In such cases, when the other person happens to be possessed of a more persistent will to do the little things in their own way, you have found it easier to let them proceed in that way—this notwithstanding that you assert your will readily enough in the greater issues of life. There is a possible danger in allowing the will to acquire too readily the habit of deferring to the will of others through repeated lack of assertion in the little things. A little vigorous exercise along these lines, once in a while, will act like a tonic to the will and keep it in good condition.

In exercise of this kind, you should employ your will to assert itself not because of any particular or direct benefit to be derived by securing the thing or action insisted upon, but solely as an exercise of the will itself, and in the direction of establishing the habit of victory for it. In fact, in such exercises you should select something in which nothing of real value is involved—something of "no consequence." The exercise should proceed absolutely along the lines of "the will to will," and not along those of the pursuit and attainment of something desired for itself. It should be like a physical exercise pursued solely for the purpose of developing and strengthening the muscles, and not for that of performing useful work or attaining some actual desired object.

Here, a word of caution is needed. Do not make the mistake of asserting your will wantonly, or for the purpose of overriding and humiliating others needlessly. Again, do not use it to create for yourself the reputation of being stubborn or unreasonable, or for having your own way regardless of the rights of others. Avoid all exercises that will attract attention to yourself or to your motives in the matter—you will find enough opportunities to exercise in this way without this drawback. Finally, do not insist upon having your way in the little things when by so doing you jeopardize having your way in the greater things in view; equally, do not insist upon having your way if your own way is the wrong way and the other way is the right one.

Mix common sense and fair play in this exercise of the will—the exercise will be all the better because of this. But, with the above cautions in mind, get into the habit of having your own way in the little, unimportant things, at least once in a while, just to get the habit well established and to keep the machinery of will well-oiled and running smoothly. Do not let your will get rusty, or gummed up, through disuse and lack of exercise.

BRACING THE WILL WITH AFFIRMATIONS

You will find it beneficial to follow the method of *bracing the will with affirmations* of its own powers and possibilities. Affirmations and statements of this kind act as a veritable will tonic and invigorator. Along these lines you may use with effect the poem by Ella Wheeler Wilcox, quoted in Chapter 1 of this book; also the quotations given in Chapter 6 of this book, in which are expressed the thoughts of some of the great human minds concerning willpower and its possibilities. All of these quotations have been selected with some particular important point in view.

You may also employ in this way the *master formula of attainment*:

1. Definite Ideals

2. Insistent Desire

3. Confident Expectations

4. Persistent Determination

5. Balanced Compensation

Likewise, the slogan, "I can, I will; I dare, I do!" You might add to the list any favorite quotations of your own, provided that they serve to inspire, energize, and strengthen your purposeful determination and to awaken the will consciousness. Finally, you will do well to add to the list the quotation from Lummis at the end of Chapter 8.

The method of procedure here is as follows: Read over each selected quotation until you have extracted its full spirit and essence and have "caught the thought" of its originator. Then carefully and thoroughly memorize it, so that you will be able to recall it readily and without undue effort—you must know it by heart as well as you do the words of your favorite song or verse. Take plenty of time for the task; but do not drop it until completed. Do not take up a second selection until you have thoroughly mastered and completed the first.

After you have these affirmative selections at your command, get into the habit of recalling them to memory from time to time. Do this at any time of the day when you have a few moments to spare—while on the subway, while walking along the street, while waiting in the hotel lobby for someone, while waiting for your train in the station, etc. Meditate upon them; get the inspiration and power from them. Also, at night, just before going to sleep, recall these quotations, one at a time, and fall asleep thinking about them. If you should happen to awaken in the middle of the night, don't worry about loss of sleep or be filled with the fear of insomnia—instead, let your mind play with these affirmative statements, and allow your soul to bathe itself in their spirit.

GENERAL SUGGESTIONS CONCERNING WILL TRAINING

In addition to the special exercises and methods of will training I have just recommended to you, you will find it useful to invent and to construct exercises of your own designed for the same end—or to create variations or combinations of the exercises and methods. Any and all forms of will-exercises are beneficial, providing that they set before the will a clearly defined task that is not beyond the powers of the aroused will to accomplish if the will sets itself earnestly to the task of accomplishing it. It is absolutely essential that the will should face the task bravely and resolutely determine to accomplish it fully.

The exercise must also always call for effort on the part of the will, if the will is expected to benefit by it. An occasional, isolated effort benefits the will little; repeated and reiterated effort is required. Particularly beneficial are regularly repeated efforts conducted on a definite method and calling forth the release of willpower in an almost habitual manner. In such exercises, you will do well to focus your willpower and to concentrate it upon some one end. Cultivate the habit of concentrated will-action in your exercises. Form a strong, definite purposeful determination, and then pour into its manifestation the whole power of your will—for the time being, let that one purposeful determination be your dominant motive and its manifestation your chief aim in life.

The successful performance of these exercises will create in you the habit of accomplishing your definite object—the custom of getting the thing done—the fashion of carrying out your determined plan. In this way, your will acquires a new confidence in itself—it acquires the habit of succeeding. It will approach more difficult tasks with a new spirit of confidence and expectation of success. A bolder and braver spirit will animate it, and it will proceed to the new and more difficult task with the spirit of the conqueror. It will have learned how to grapple with a difficult situation as earnestly as one does with a physical enemy. It will proceed to the combat with that tenacity of determination, with that fierceness of resolve, with that passion for success which a writer has well said "may almost be called vindictive" in its aggressive and persistent quality.

Do not let the apparent triviality of the tasks cause you to undervalue their importance in your will training. As has well been said: "Willpower is built up by a gradual process of practice on the smallest things, and every act of self-conquest in one sphere of life makes the battle easier in all the other spheres." Persistently conducted exercises of this kind, inspired by the determination to gain strength and power of will, and its definite direction and control, will inevitably lead to that which you seek to gain. But, as a celebrated teacher has added: "Will-exercises must be methodical and well-regulated as to degree and length, or else they are perhaps worse than useless."

I don't need to remind you that there is no exclusive virtue in any of the particular tasks I have suggested for your practice and exercise. You may substitute almost any others for them, and, in fact, you will do well to use your ingenuity and powers of invention in that direction. The one thing you must always observe is that the particular principles I mentioned must always be involved in your exercises. Again, you may exercise along the lines either 1) of performing some positive actions during a certain fixed time; or else 2) of avoiding some particular actions during such time. The one is a positive form of exercise, the other is the negative form.

THE NEW MOTIVE

When you have learned to perform the will training exercises, you will have made an interesting discovery concerning your feelings, impulses, desires, and will-action. Before, you performed your will-actions solely by reason of the push or pull of some strong feeling or desire; and you have seen that all will-action is caused, directly or indirectly, by feeling and desire. Now, in the performance of these exercises, you will have found that you are acting apparently without the push or pull of feeling or desire—in fact, in several of the exercises you will be actually acting against such push or pull. Then, you may well ask: "What is the motive of my action? What is its motive cause?" Here, at this point, you make a discovery.

You will find that you have aroused within yourself the will-feeling, the will-desire, the will-impulse—those strange emotional states that are satisfied and contented solely by the exercise of the will for the mere sake of willing, without regard to the intrinsic value of the act. You here make the acquaintance of *the will to will*—that unique mental state that seems to arise at the very center of your mental being, deeper than any feeling, any emotion, any desire, any impulse. Here, the will is willing to will, moved only by will, and gratifying only will. This strange mental state is definable only in its own terms—there is nothing else with which to compare it, nothing with which to define it. It must be experienced in order to be understood—but once experienced, you will never forget it.

If you are interested in this newly discovered mental state, which I trust you have already found manifesting in yourself, I strongly advise you to consider carefully the following section of this book. In it you will learn about your new feeling and consciousness in further detail. If you have not already made this interesting and important discovery in yourself, you may now be on the verge of it; if so, the following section entitled "Will Consciousness" may perhaps hasten the hour of your deliverance and make easier your new birth into dynamic willpower. The man or woman who experiences will consciousness is reborn in will—this time into the world of the *will to will*, in which the mastery of will is the normal condition and the habitual state.

CHAPTER 8

WILL
CONSCIOUSNESS

That there is a state of consciousness called the *will consciousness*—a state in which the will becomes conscious of its own existence, its powers, its possibilities—is a fact thoroughly attested by the actual experience of many individuals. Yet to those who have not as yet entered into this conscious experience, there is no way of proving its validity and, indeed, no words adequate to express or define it.

The experience of will consciousness is akin to that experience of full self-consciousness, which comes to many people at some time in life, but which remains but a name to others. Or, again, it is akin to the dawn of aesthetic sense that often suddenly bursts into consciousness in favored individuals, enabling them to experience beauty as with a new sense, and which, when once experienced, can never be entirely forgotten or lost.

But, on the other hand, will consciousness is different from those two somewhat analogous experiences. Those particular experiences are characterized by a sense of individual existence and real being, in the first case, and by a sense of added perception, in the second case. Will consciousness, however, is characterized by the recognition of self-power, realization of self-action, and manifestation of freedom of expression, accompanied by the thrill of the feeling of self-mastery—by the inner certainty of mastery over outer things, which arises from the consciousness of the possession of these self-powers.

In the full state of will consciousness, the awareness of power, freedom, and ability to act is accompanied by a peculiar "feeling" that is most difficult to describe, but is quite apparent to those who have experienced it in even a faint degree. Some psychologists have called it *will feeling*, for want of a better name. This will feeling is experienced in every true will-action, but reaches the stage of emotion only when the will *wills to will* for the sake of willing, particularly when in doing so it sets aside the strenuous push or pull of ordinary feeling and desire. In such cases, it is as if the will has ascended to a higher plane of consciousness, leaving the feelings and desires behind on the lower planes.

You will experience this will feeling most keenly when you proceed to manifest your willpower in the face of obstacles and hindrances. It will arouse in you the thrill of courage and daring—the enthusiasm of bravery. You will find that as you develop and train your will you will open the door to an entirely new phase of satisfying and contenting emotion—a phase that seems to develop along the lines of will-development and training. It never fades nor grows stale; on the contrary, it grows steadily until finally it becomes one of the dominant elements or factors of your emotional life.

In its highest stages, this will consciousness will seem to wear thin the barrier that separates your individual self from what may be called the will of the *all-power*—that ultimate power which is the source and origin of all the power manifested in the universe. In this stage, you will at times become dimly aware of the throb of the heart of the universe—will feel its energies pulsing through your mental and spiritual arteries. At such moments you will become aware that "The All is One, and each is a part, and not apart as it seemed to be; the heart of life has a single beat, pulsing through God, and clod, and *me!*" In this dawn of the will consciousness there will come to you a sense of joy and of a peace that indeed "passeth all understanding."

The will consciousness cannot be purchased with money; neither can it be acquired as a gift from others. It must be acquired by work and exercise, by a steadfast development of your own inherent powers. You learn to will to will only by willing; and you acquire will consciousness only by

willing to will. By your own efforts you must arouse the
sleeping giant within yourself; and by your own efforts you
must awaken to a conscious realization of your own existence and power. When you have done this, then someday
it will suddenly dawn upon you that this giant will is really
yourself—your greater self that has swallowed up the old
partial manifestation of selfhood you formerly regarded as
your self.

From the very dawn of will consciousness, you will
become aware that you are a master, and no longer a slave.
You will experience a sense of freedom and independence
and will be able to see what a puppet-like creature you formerly were. Having escaped from the control of the lesser
desires and impulses (by having entered into the spirit
of the greater), you will find that these lesser desires and
impulses now will rally around your standard, will give you
allegiance, will swear fealty to you; for, from the moment
you have conquered them, they will become your eager and
earnest servants. Despise not these lesser elements of feeling, desire, and impulse—they will prove useful servants
to you, so set them to work for you. Feeling, impulse, and
desire, like fire, are good servants, though poor masters.
Remember the old aphorism: "All things are good enough
to be used by you; but no thing is good enough to use you."

It is a platitude that "a person who gains self-mastery
attains to the mastery of others"; but only when you have
developed willpower and attained will consciousness are

you able to read the full meaning in these old and familiar words. Only then will you perceive the truth of the teachings of the ancient sages who held that you may exert the mastery over other people and things—even over wild beasts and natural forces—but you must first have gained the mastery over the rebellious elements of your own nature, which have usurped the throne that is rightfully your own.

When you have conquered the inner forces, you have acquired the right to control the outer forces. When you have deposed the usurpers of your kingdom and have seated yourself upon the inner throne of your own mental and spiritual being, then will you be able to issue your edicts to the outer kingdom over which you have sovereignty. When you have tamed and mastered the menagerie of wild beasts within yourself, then will you be able to master and control the wild beasts in others. So said the ancient teachers; the best modern thought sustains the doctrine.

There is a serious side to this attainment, however, which you must not fail to recognize and to heed. In attaining this reward of willpower and will consciousness, you will find in your hands a mighty instrument for good or for evil. There will come to you at times a sense of tremendous responsibility for the proper use of this new-found power—the greater the degree of power you attain, the greater is your responsibility. Your resolutions will lose their former character of impermanency and ineffectiveness—they will take on the character of permanent, effective forces. They will become deeply rooted in and strongly attached to reality; they will become terribly sincere and real—at times you may actually experience awe when you contemplate them.

At times, there may come to you the temptation to regard yourself as apart from other people who have not as yet attained the heights you have reached. These other people will show that they recognize something different in you and will fail to understand you. They may even feel uncomfortable in your presence and be apt to regard you as cold, unsympathetic, or even as lacking in some of the qualities of humanity. This is because you have risen above some of the common weaknesses of humanity in its present stage of development and evolution. You will find yourself, in a sense, living "ahead of your time." There will be manifest in you the prophecy and the dawning spirit of the super-human. Be not unduly affected by these things; keep in touch with the world as it is; retain your sympathy with humankind as it is; and, above all, keep your feet on the ground of practical everyday life in the present, and be not tempted to soar up to the region of the clouds—one plane at a time, remember!

You will discover that when you have developed and trained your will—when you have acquired willpower and have attained the will consciousness—you will have become more truly an individual than you were before. You will have become a master of destiny instead of remaining a slave of circumstance. You will know what you can do, and you will do it. You will be able to do what you will, and to will that which you do. You will have mastered both impulse and lethargy; you will have reached the Golden Mean between the two extremes. You will possess and use energy, yet will not needlessly and uselessly waste or dissipate it. You will be able to begin a task, to continue it as far as is necessary, and to discontinue it when wisdom dictates that course. You will be able to proceed just as far as is required—yet will be able to stop at that point and not take an unnecessary step.

You will also find that you have no inclination to air and display your new-found power for the edification or mystification of others. You will possess that certain sense of inherent power that will cause you to rise above such weaknesses and vain displays. The truly strong person does not boast of their strength and power; neither do they vaingloriously strive to exhibit it. You will be aware that others recognize the power within you and are influenced by it, yet that very sense of the possession of certain power will tend to inhibit you from boasting about or making a needless display of it. You will realize that willpower does not manifest itself in gritting the teeth, clenching the fists, protruding the chest like a pouter-pigeon, or heaving the bosom like the movie heroine "registering" emotion.

Likewise, you will discover for yourself that which all wise people, of all ages and all lands, have always known—that willpower and will consciousness do not necessarily impart gruffness, sternness, nor harshness to their possessor. True willpower frequently screens itself with an exterior of suavity and agreeableness. Many individuals of the strongest willpower manifest a pleasant manner and express a suave politeness to such a degree that the unthinking observer may be deceived into believing that the individual has no will of their own, and that their only desire and object in life is that of being agreeable and pleasant to others. But when the opportunity presents itself, these individuals manifest fully and unmistakably the latent strength within themselves. The "iron hand in the velvet glove" is the ideal of the diplomat; and men like Talleyrand possessed this quality in a remarkable degree, as history records. The blusterers and braggarts usually are found to possess no real power.

Finally, you will discover that the figurative expression in which the strong will is called the "iron will" is imperfect. You will find that this figure of speech does not convey the idea of what the strongly developed and scientifically trained will really is. In its place, you will prefer to use the expression "the steel will"—the will of finely tempered steel.

The iron will may break under the strain of circumstances, whereas the will of steel will yield a little for the moment, only to spring back to its original position and form when the pressure is withdrawn. The steel will bends at times, rather than allowing itself to be broken; but it always springs back, in true form, and resumes its action inspired by purposeful determination. The steel will bends—but it never loses its shape, form, or strength. Its purpose may be frustrated temporarily, but it is never permanently defeated. In fact, the energy of its rebound and springing-back often serves to accomplish the desired end and purpose. Think of your will as being like the thoroughly tempered, fine, strong Damascus blade that bends and springs back when necessary—but which is never broken nor bent out of shape—rather than as the iron bar that breaks under pressure or else is bent out of shape.

Summing up the discoveries you make when you have developed and trained your willpower until you experience at least the dawn of will consciousness and the *will to will*, you will find that you have acquired the following qualities, attributes, and powers:

1. The consciousness of pure will within yourself;

2. The habit of employing that will with directness, efficiency, and scientific accuracy;

3. The knowledge of an inexhaustible mine of inner resources, power, and ability to act with purposeful determination.

4. The power to will to will for the sake of will consciousness.

5. The power of manifesting or inhibiting will-action by will.

Better than all, you will have discovered that at the very center and heart of your will—on the very throne of will—*you*, yourself, abide as the sovereign ruler. When you have reached the ultimate stage of will consciousness, lo! Will itself will seem to have disappeared, and *you* alone will remain—then your will will have become the "acting part" of your self! Emerson says it well: "There can be no driving force except through the conversion of the man into his will, making him the will, and the will him!"

I know of no better words to pass on to you as the keynote of what I have sought to teach you in this chapter than the statement of Charles F. Lummis, who summed up in the following words the result of his own experience of a life of conflict in which he emerged a victor over strong odds:

> The great lesson all this has taught me is that man was meant to be, and ought to be, stronger and more than anything that can happen to him. Circumstances, fate, luck, are all outside; and if he cannot change them, he can always beat them. If it had not worked its way into my broken brain that Captain "I" held the fort; that the only key was my own will, and that unless I willfully surrendered nothing could take the citadel, I should have been dead long ago. …I am all right. I am bigger than anything that can happen to me. All these things are outside my door—and I've got the key.

CHAPTER 9

WILL
ATMOSPHERE

T he individual in whom the will consciousness has been unfolded and manifested—who has learned how to will to will—is usually found to have unconsciously developed that peculiar aura, field of emanation, or whatever else it may be called, which is known to close students of the subject as the *will atmosphere.* The will atmosphere is like the "field of induction" of the strong magnet, the forces of which influence the particles of iron or steel within its limits. The will atmosphere of the will-conscious individual exerts a subtle but most powerful influence over those with whom they come in contact. In some strange way, the other people coming within the "field of induction" of such an individual instinctively recognize the power latent within their region of will, and they consciously or unconsciously adapt themselves to it.

I wish here to illustrate this principle of will atmosphere by citing several celebrated cases in which the force in question has been manifested in a striking manner. For some of these illustrations I am indebted to Dr. J. Milner Fothergill, who, a number of years ago, gathered together many instances and examples of willpower and included them in *The Will Power: Its Range in Action*.

First of all, I ask you to consider that striking illustration given by Oliver Wendell Holmes, which Fothergill prefaces with the following comment:

> The steady conflict of the eye is familiar to many of us. The boy looks at his mother to see if she is in earnest in her threat; when older he likewise looks at his schoolmaster to read his purpose. Two men or women look at each other steadily; no word is said; yet the conflict is over soon, and one walks ahead of the other ever after. The instance related by Holmes is stated by him as follows: The Koh-i-noor's face turned so white with rage that his blue-black mustache and beard looked fearful seen against it. He grinned with wrath, and caught at a tumbler, as if he would have thrown its contents at the speaker. The young Marylander fixed his clear steady eye upon him, and laid his hand on his arm, carelessly almost, but the Jewel felt it was held so that he could not move it. It was of no use. The youth was his master in muscle, and in

that deadly Indian hug in which men wrestle with their eyes, over in five seconds, but breaks one of their two backs, and is good for three-score years and ten, one trial enough—settles the whole matter—just as when two feathered songsters of the barnyard, game and dunghill, come together. After a jump or two at each other, and a few sharp kicks, there is an end of it; and it is "*Aprés vous, Monsieur,*" with the beaten party in all the social relations for all the rest of his days.Fothergill relates with relish the celebrated instance of the meeting of Hugo, Bishop of Lincoln, and Richard Coeur de Lion in the Church of Roche d'Andeli. In this case, Richard, being involved in war with Normandy, demanded more supplies of his barons. The bishop of Lincoln refused to supply any men, holding that the see of Lincoln was bound to military service only when the war was waged within the four seas of Britain. Richard, a man of very strong will, was incensed by the refusal of the bishop and summoned the latter to Normandy.

When the bishop reached Normandy, he found that the king was furiously enraged with him; mutual friends advised him to send a conciliatory message to the king before venturing to enter his presence. But the bishop declined the advice and preferred to trust to his own sense of awakened will consciousness.

157

The king was sitting at mass when the prelate walked up to him and, despite the monarch's frown, said, "Kiss me, my lord king!" The king turned away his face. Hugo shook him, and repeated his request. "Thou hast not deserved it," growled the king fiercely. "I have," returned the undaunted prelate, shaking the king by the shoulder even still harder. The king yielded, the kiss was given; and the bishop passed calmly on to take part in the service.

Fothergill adds:Mere indifference to death could never have produced such a result. There was something more. As well as being utterly fearless, Bishop Hugo possessed a will-power of most unusual character, of which several instances are on record. Not only did he face the king and justify his refusal to supply men in the council chamber afterwards; he went further, and rebuked [the king] for infidelity to his queen. "The Lion was tamed for the moment. The king acknowledged nothing, but restrained his passion, observing afterwards, 'If all bishops were like my lord of Lincoln not a prince among us could lift his head against them.'" Such is the story as told by Froude. Yet Richard was the last man to permit a liberty to be taken with him, as his whole history showed.This, however, was not the only instance in the career of Hugo in which he showed that his willpower was capable of dominating that of his king. An earlier king, Henry Plantagenet, who, indeed, had made Hugo the bishop of Lincoln in the first place, went down in defeat before the bishop's willpower, as truly as did his successor. King Henry requested a favor to be bestowed by the bishop upon a certain courtier; his request was bluntly refused. Hugo had already braved the wrath of the king, and the monarch was very angry at him. Fothergill says:

> Henry was with his suite in Woodstock Park, and sat down on the ground pretending to be mending his glove when the bishop approached him. The king took no notice of his spiritual peer. After a brief pause, Hugo pushing aside an earl sat down by the king's side. Watching the royal proceedings, he remarked: "Your Highness reminds me of your cousins at Falaise." Falaise was famous for its leather work, and it was at Falaise Duke Robert met Arlotta, the tanner's daughter, the mother of William the Conqueror [King Henry's ancestor]. The reference to his humble ancestry was too much for the king, who was utterly worsted in the discussion which followed.

> A similar character is presented to us at the present day in General Gordon. It was not his absolute indifference about his life which gained him his ascendency. In China where life is held to be of little or no moment, the absence of any fear of death would go but little way, and did not constitute the basis of Chinese Gordon's ascendency; his secret lay elsewhere. Nor did his supremacy in the Soudan rest upon his bravery; for the Arabs of the Soudan are as brave as any

warriors in the world, as our recent contests there conflicts testify. When Gordon took a chair and sate himself down by King John of Abyssinia, or presented himself alone to the Arab sheiks who had sworn to take his life, it was not his disdain of death alone which carried him through both perils unharmed, or enabled him to hold Khartoum. Equally implicit confidence in the protection of heaven has not saved others when in peril.

All the faith of Savonarola only led him to a horrible death amidst torturing flames. But without this indifference to their fate neither Bishop Hugo nor General Gordon could have come unscathed out of the terrible dangers they deliberately chose to meet. Any fear of death certainly would emasculate any man under these circumstances. The will must be accompanied by personal courage when danger to life has to be encountered. The heroism of the Jesuits, who labored among the Red Indians early in the history of Canada, was sustained by their devotion, for many suffered terrible cruelties. But no one of them ever possessed in a higher degree that will-power which compels the obedience of others than did La Salle, the pioneer of the Mississippi. In George Washington we see a splendid illustration of that power which molds other men, and compels them to follow its behests. His patient sagacity rested on the basis of his will-force.

A curious instance of the magnetic power of will was furnished by the story of the relations of the late Benjamin Disraeli to the Conservative party in England. An alien, handicapped by his early avocations, at first the House refused to listen to him. Yet irresistibly he rose step by step to be a Conservative leader who "educated" his party; and at last was prime minister with a solid array of the best-bred Norman-descended patricians of England at his back, yielding ready obedience to his wishes; a leader of men—men, too, deeply imbued with traditions: and also a personal friend of his sovereign. Here what is meant by the words, "By faith ye shall move mountains," was illustrated vividly.

The House of Orange has furnished some striking examples of the effect of the will. William the Silent held his followers together by an iron will that bent under no catastrophe, no disaster. It refused to submit. A like character was that of William, afterwards king of England. Men who disliked him did his bidding. He inspired the dispirited allies with his own resoluteness. When his schemes were foiled by a defeat, he immediately set to work to repair his losses, and deprive the French of the fruit of their victory. That the

house of Orange possessed many grand characteristics will be readily admitted; but no one of
their endowments is more remarkable than their
power of will.

The peculiar commanding power of leaders, no
matter whether regular like John Churchill; or
that of a guerrilla chief like Mina, in the Pen-
insula war of Spain; of the Red Indian Pontiac,
who imperiled the existence of the Anglo-Saxons
on the American continent; or even the negro
commander Toussaint l'Ouverture, seems not to
depend upon ability only: but upon character
in which the will-force is a leading factor. Men
with marked will-power come to the front in
emergencies, as seen in Oliver Cromwell, the
fen grazier; and Napoleon Bonaparte, the artil-
lery subaltern. In both these instances national
convulsions produced the seething caldron from
whence they rose; each to an eminence of position and fame. They were heavily handicapped by
their early position, yet they rose superior to it.
But amidst all these men there rises up a woman
even more remarkable than they—La Pucell, the
village maiden, Joan of Arc, who inspired courage into the beaten warriors of France, and led
them to victory. ...In what lay her witchcraft [for
which she was finally burnt]? In her capacity to
animate others: which was really based on her

will-power! The case of Disraeli, mentioned above by Fothergill, is a typical instance of the possession of "that something"—combined willpower and will atmosphere—which distinguishes individuals in whom the will consciousness has been awakened and developed. When he first arose to speak in the House of Commons, he was jeered and derided—the House would have none of him. Upon this occasion he hurled at his opponents that remarkable prophecy: "I have begun several times many things, and I have often succeeded at last; aye! and though I may sit down now, the time will come when you will hear me!" And that time did come—and before long, too.

Fothergill says of this:

The time came, sure enough, when the House not only listened to him, but even acknowledged his mastery over it. Disraeli had learned, what many another man learns, that because he failed at first it does not follow that ultimate success is unattainable. …The baffled speaker came to be able to hold the House spell-bound with his barbed shafts of rhetoric. He soon attacked fiercely Sir Robert Peel, who was an excellent speaker; and the pungency of his remarks taught the House to dread him—at whom they once had scoffed!

It must have needed great resolution to face the House of Commons again after that first terrible rebuff; but after the attempt had once been made, the rest was comparatively easy. Disraeli's subsequent career furnishes one of the most striking examples of the power of the individual to overcome apparently insurmountable obstacles by sheer force of willpower. Step by step he advanced in face of opposition sufficient to have dismayed any ordinary person. At last, he, Disraeli the Jew, became Prime Minister of England and the actual ruler of the destinies of a great part of the world.

This man has thrilled the souls of several later generations of courageous and ambitious people, not only by the force of his example, but also by those remarkable words of his, but which I wish here to impress still more forcibly upon your memory: "I have brought myself by long meditation to the conviction that a human being with a settled purpose must accomplish it, and that nothing can resist a will which will stake even existence itself upon its fulfillment."

It is not only the history of warfare and statesmanship that is filled with instances in which willpower, will consciousness, and will atmosphere have won the day—the history of business likewise is rich in examples of this kind.

A study of the life histories of the great captains of industry, of those who "have arrived" in the various fields of business life, will convince any unprejudiced reader that there exists a "something" which exerts its forces and energies in favor of the individual possessing it. A still closer analysis will reveal the fact that "that something" has willpower at the very heart and center of itself, is possessed of the will consciousness, and manifests the will atmosphere.

Fothergill gives us many instances of this kind in his study of the history of English manufacturers. I shall give you in brief form a statement of several of the most typical of these cases; a study of these and similar cases serves to awaken your perhaps dormant willpower and also illustrates the general principle now under consideration.

Josiah Wedgwood was the youngest of fourteen children, bred and born a potter. At that time the pottery business of England was limited to a very common earthenware; the fine pottery now produced is largely the result of the pioneer work performed by this one-time little delicate lad. He was apprenticed to the trade, but was handicapped by illness, which made him lame in his right knee and finally resulted in the amputation of his right leg. Crippled as he was, he worked away. Gladstone afterward said of him that his physical disability "sent his mind inwards, and drove him to meditate upon the laws and secrets of his art."

By adding silica to the clay, he succeeded in making a white ware instead of the dirty-colored products hitherto made. Then he began to experiment along the lines of perfecting his glazes. Then he had to erect his furnaces. Then came the art taste. He paid large sums for old examples of art ware and copied these accurately. Then he re-discovered the lost art of painting on "biscuit ware" practiced by the old Etruscans, and then employed Flaxman as his artist. He worked for the throne and became the "royal potter." He not only advanced himself, but also made in his part of England a great high-grade pottery producing center. Wedgewood furnishes a typical example of the person handicapped by nature, facing great obstacles, meeting with many discouragements, but in the end triumphing by means of the consistent application of his willpower. In him the will consciousness had been awakened—he had the will atmosphere highly developed, according to the testimony of those of his own times.

The story of Lister and "silk waste" also furnishes an illustration of the general principle under consideration. Lister's attention was directed to what was known as *silk waste*—the waste made from the manufacture of neat silk and pierced cocoons, and which looked like mutilated ropes, dirty flocks, or mucilaginous hemp, and was knotted and sticky and choked with sticks and leaves and dead silkworms. For many years he struggled with the problem of converting this unpromising waste stuff into available silk material. He battled with circumstances and repeatedly faced utter financial ruin in the attempt.

At one time he was out of pocket no less a sum than $1,500,000, the fortune previously made by him in other ventures. His indomitable will, his unflagging energy, and his persistent endeavors alone carried him through and converted defeat into victory. In the end, he succeeded in manufacturing silk velvets, velvets with a silk pile and cotton back, silk carpets, imitation sealskin, plush velvet ribbons, corded ribbons, sewing silks, Japanese silks, poplins, etc. from the once despised silk waste. When, in after years, a statue to Lister was unveiled at Bradford, England, an eminent speaker said: "What is it especially we are honoring? It is the pluck which this man has shown; it is the feeling that he said to himself, 'here is something which ought to be done; I will not rest until I have found out how it can be done, and having found out how it can be done, where is the man who will stop me doing it?'"

A writer relating the story of Josiah Mason, the English manufacturer who started in business at the age of eight years peddling cakes on the street and who, when he died, was one of Great Britain's great commercial giants, says of the subject of his sketch:

Mason had, to begin with, a strong, powerful, almost irresistible will. That which he wanted, he would have; and in a great measure he did have. Little or great, all objects or purposes came within the range of his powerful will. And whatever or whoever he opposed, he surely conquered in the end. Not that he was blindly obstinate, or unwilling to take counsel. Another great quality which he possessed—very helpful to the accomplishment of his will—was absolute patience. He knew how to wait. With patience there went in close union a wonderful perseverance. Mason was remarkably tenacious. He held firm to his purpose, and worked it out with never-ceasing vigilance and energy. He was the embodiment of living willpower.Illustrations and examples of this kind might be multiplied indefinitely. The story is the same, no matter of whom it is told, or what may be the native land of that person. It becomes certain to the student of the subject that some great, general, universal principle is behind these manifold instances. There is always evident the presence and power of "that something" which is manifesting as willpower, will consciousness, will atmosphere. The matter is raised out of the category of mere coincidence by the overwhelming number of the cases in which the principle is found operating. It is the result of an invariable process of cause and effect—of the law of causation operating on the plane of mentality.

I believe that the principles and methods I have set forth in the pages of this book will serve to point out to the earnest, persistent, courageous individual the road you must travel in your journey toward attainment by willpower. I believe that in the statement of the master formula is to be found the secret of success. Let me repeat it to you once more in its popular form. Here it is: "You may have anything you want, provided that you know exactly what you want, want it hard enough, confidently expect to obtain it, persistently determine to attain it, and are willing to pay the price of its attainment."

Re-read the instances of success through willpower related in the previous pages of this chapter, and consider them in the light of the master formula of attainment above. You will see that in each and every case the successful individual has, first, known exactly what they wanted to do or to get; they have then wanted it hard enough; they have firmly believed in and confidently expected to get or to do it; they have persistently determined to get or to do it; and, finally, they have always been willing to "pay the price" of the will-atmosphere attainment or achievement. In each case there has been that marked manifestation of 1) ideals, 2) desire, 3) faith, 4) will, and 5) service.

Let us close by quoting the following truths from the writing of Dr. Fothergill, that esteemed pioneer in the work of recording the principles and practice of willpower, whose work has served as at least a part of the foundation structure of all who have followed him. He says:

Willpower is seen in the man who bides his time, who knows how to wait—which involves the "when" and the "why." Circumstances may stand in his way, and he must wait; but the will is neither bent, broken, nor warped by that fact, and is all along as assertive as ever—even when apparently in abeyance. Yet willpower is not mere perseverance; it is something more. It is an entity in itself!

WILLIAM WALKER ATKINSON

illiam Walker Atkinson (1862–1932) was an influential American author, lawyer, and pioneer of the New Thought movement. A prolific writer, Atkinson authored over 100 books under various pseudonyms, including Yogi Ramacharaka and Theron Q. Dumont, exploring topics such as the power of the mind, personal development, and the laws of attraction. His works, including the widely read *The Kybalion* and *Thought Vibration*, have inspired millions to harness the latent powers of the mind and live a life of greater success and fulfillment. Atkinson's legacy continues to resonate with readers seeking to unlock their potential through the mastery of thought and willpower.

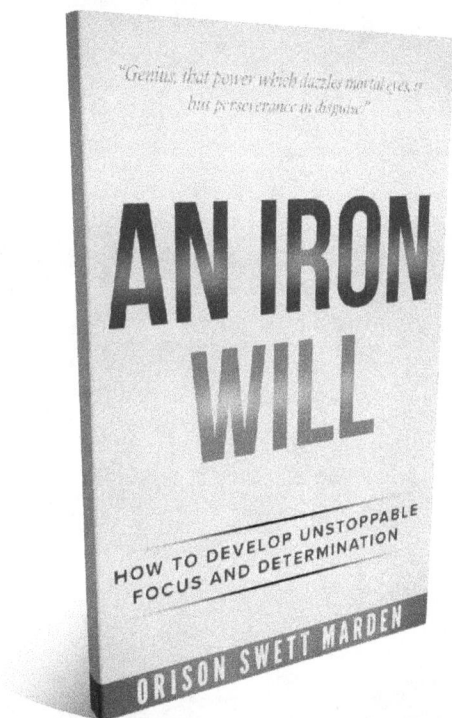

THANK YOU FOR READING THIS BOOK!

If you found any of the information helpful, please take a few minutes and leave a review on the bookselling platform of your choice.

BONUS GIFT!

Don't forget to sign up to try our newsletter and grab your free personal development ebook here:

soundwisdom.com/classics

sound wisdom®

Because Your Success Matters

www.ingramcontent.com/pod-product-compliance
Lightning Source LLC
Chambersburg PA
CBHW072347090426
42741CB00012B/2956